Living the Mysteries

Living the Mysteries
A Guide for Unfinished Christians

Scott Hahn

Mike Aquilina

Our Sunday Visitor Publishing Division
Our Sunday Visitor, Inc.
Huntington, IN 46750

Nihil Obstat: Rev. Daniel J. Maurer, S.T.L.
Censor Deputatus
Imprimatur: Donald W. Wuerl, S.T.D.
Bishop of Pittsburgh
May 8, 2003

The *Nihil Obstat* and *Imprimatur* are declarations that a work is considered free from doctrinal or moral error. It is not implied that those who have granted the same agree with the contents, opinions, or statements expressed.

Unless otherwise indicated, Scripture excerpts used in this work are taken from the *Catholic Edition of the Revised Standard Version of the Bible* (RSV), copyright © 1965 and 1966 by the Division of Christian Education of the National Council of the Churches of Christ in the United States of America. Used by permission. All rights reserved. Some Scripture excerpts are taken from the *New American Bible with Revised New Testament and Psalms* (NAB), copyright © 1991, 1986, 1970, Confraternity of Christian Doctrine, Inc., Washington, D.C. Used with permission. All rights reserved. No part of the *New American Bible* may be reproduced by any means without permission in writing from the copyright owner. Still other excerpts are from *Confraternity of Christian Doctrine* (CCD); and the *Douay-Rheims* (DR). Catechism excerpts are from the English translation of the *Catechism of the Catholic Church, Second Edition,* for use in the United States of America, copyright © 1994 and 1997, United States Catholic Conference — Libreria Editrice Vaticana. Used by permission. All rights reserved.

Every reasonable effort has been made to determine copyright holders of excerpted materials and to secure permissions as needed. If any copyrighted materials have been inadvertently used in this work without proper credit being given in one form or another, please notify Our Sunday Visitor in writing so that future printings of this work may be corrected accordingly.

ISBN: 1-931709-12-2 (Inventory No. T11) LCCN: 2003105339
Cover design by Monica Haneline / Interior design by Sherri L. Hoffman
Cover image compliments of Saint Isaac of Syria Skete, www.skete.com.
PRINTED IN THE UNITED STATES OF AMERICA

Contents

❧

CHAPTER 1

On Unfinished Christians

Not long ago, a series of self-help books appeared. The series was called *Teach Yourself.* And its titles made extravagant promises: *Teach Yourself Basketball, Teach Yourself Jazz Piano,* and *Teach Yourself Plumbing.* One title, however, was the most outlandish of all: *Teach Yourself Christianity.*

Maybe the author intended the title to be ironic. Indeed, there is no other way it could make sense. For one of the first things anyone must learn about Christianity is that it cannot be self-taught. There are no "self-made" success stories in the spiritual life, no do-it-yourself kits for aspiring saints or self-help manuals for authentic mystical experience. "How can they hear without someone to preach?" asked St. Paul. "And how can people preach unless they are sent?" (Rom 10:14-15, NAB). Those words imply a Church with authority to send and to preach; they imply a doctrine, a way of preaching, and a manner of hearing.

The early Church had a process by which seekers found a teacher, and the teacher guided them gradually through stages of inquiry, purification, and illumination. The process could take several years, and it culminated in a final phase called mystagogy (pronounced MIST-a-go-gee), which means the "revelation of the mysteries." What are the "mysteries" revealed in mystagogy? The mysteries are the sacraments, which are themselves revelations of God's eternal mystery that surpasses all understanding (see Eph 3:19). Everything in the earthly life of Jesus was a sign of that mystery (see CCC, n. 515); and now, in the age of the Church, the mysteries of Christ's life have passed over into the sacramental mysteries.

As the last phase of initiation, mystagogy came only after the seeker was no longer a seeker, but a Christian — newborn to divine life in baptism and made one with Christ in Holy Communion. Indeed, all the previous stages served as needed preparation for the last. Only a purified mind and body could be worthy vessels of the mysteries. Only an enlightened soul could "see" the invisible reality that is present in every sacrament.

Yet it was the promise of this end that drew the seekers onward through the long and sometimes grueling course of learning and purification. The mystery of God, after all, is ultimately what attracted them to the faith, though it had been only glimpsed — as through a glass, darkly — in the rites and prayers of the Church.

Even today, what draws many people to the faith is the very stuff of mystagogy: the Church's rituals, its ancient tradition, its mystical life, its rich interpretation of the Bible, and the bold promise of communion with God. Mystagogy, then, is the fulfillment of all the teaching that has gone before, and is the only suitable conclusion to that teaching.

Mystagogy for the Masses

Still, it's fair for us to ask whether this teaching should be "for converts only." Many Catholics who were baptized as infants still feel they know too little of the Church's mystical life, or sacramental life, or biblical teaching. Even the authors of this book — one a cradle Catholic with twelve years of Catholic schooling, the other a scholar with a doctorate in theology — feel the need for ongoing mystagogy.

Mystagogy is what we all need, and what we always need, because God's mysteries are inexhaustible. Till we get to heaven, we're all unfinished Christians.

The technical definition of mystagogy is "post-baptismal instruction," and it is usually assumed that this lasts from Easter to Pentecost. But there is no reason why it cannot extend until the end of one's life on earth. After all, each and every one of those days qualifies as "post-baptismal."

In this book, we have tried to give modern readers some sense of how the ancient Christians experienced mystagogy. It was a daily event then. The newly baptized believers met by the altar every morning to listen to their bishop explain the most profound truths of the faith. You'll note, as you read, that their explanations were primarily explanations of the Scriptures. In their mystagogical teachings, the Church Fathers continued the "typological" reading of Scripture that Christ taught to His disciples — that is, they saw the New Testament concealed in the Old, and the Old Testament revealed in the New. The Fathers saw the great events of salvation history as "types" prefiguring the sacraments of the New Covenant. Peter was able to understand the great flood as a sign of baptism; Paul could see the Eucharist foreshadowed in the manna given to Israel in the desert.

A precious handful of mystagogical sermons have survived the centuries, and we have used these to prepare the daily meditations included in this book. Because the period of most intense mystagogy lasted the fifty days from Easter to Pentecost, we have included fifty readings. But the book is not designed, necessarily, to be "seasonal." Mystagogy is the work of a lifetime, and the words of the Church Fathers are always timely witnesses to the Christian meaning of current events and of our own inner lives.

Nevertheless, while the book is not seasonal, it does have a certain flow. The first meditations introduce the idea of the mysteries and the role of the Church's tradition in revealing them through the ages. Later meditations focus on the individual sacraments of Christian life, their visible rituals, their deepest roots in human history, and their deepest meaning in eternal reality. The final readings return to the idea of the mysteries, then considering them in the fullness of their heavenly glory.

So the book moves from glory to greater glory, as should our souls as we grow in grace, immerse ourselves in the sacraments, and respond to God's many mercies in the everyday (sometimes difficult) events of our lives. The mysteries are eternal; our share in them is perpetual, and it can be far richer, if we want it to be.

How to Use This Book

It is our hope that you will take these ancient readings, meditate on them in quiet moments, and let them feed your prayer throughout the day. That is why, at the end of each reading, we have highlighted a few short lines for further consideration. And from each passage we have chosen a single line to be learned by heart.

There is no certified Catholic way to meditate. But we suggest that you set aside a regular time each day, preferably a quiet time. Begin the time by acknowledging God's presence, thanking Him for His blessings, and telling Him of your love. Then, once you've told Him as much or as little as you have to say at the moment, go on to the day's meditation. But don't just read it. Go through it slowly; ponder the phrases that almost two millennia's worth of Christians have deemed to be treasures; and ask God to show you what they mean, both for you and for Him.

End your meditation at the appointed time. But try to refer back to it, briefly, throughout your day. The points for meditation might be useful. Jot them down on a piece of paper and keep them in your pocket, scribble them into your daily calendar, or tap them into your handheld or laptop computer. Try praying the line labeled "Learn It by Heart" several times during the day. Memorization can be a great way to make a spiritual doctrine your own — not only the words, but the truths, which have found immortal expression in the words of these Fathers and mystics.

Even if you read this book in the quiet of your room, do not consider it "self-help" or a "self-guided" meditation. For the mysteries cannot be self-taught. Only God can reveal them, and He has chosen to do so through those who are sent by the Church. In this book, you will encounter eight of the greatest mystical teachers of the ancient Church. Many generations of Christians have preserved the words of these masters at great cost — copying them, again and again, by hand, even risking death to safeguard the wisdom contained in their manuscripts. After almost two millennia, the words of the Fathers have proven more durable than most monuments of stone.

To those who thirst, a glass of water is more valuable than gold. Water, after all, is their only hope of life. To those who thirst for the living God, the words of mystagogy will always hold an inestimable value, more precious than gold and even earthly life itself, because they hold not just momentary refreshment, but the promise of life without end.

About the Translations

Many of the meditations in this book are actual sermons given during the weeks immediately following baptism. These, in particular, were written as "mystagogical" teaching. Other passages we chose because, whether or not they were originally preached to the newly baptized, they unveil the sacred mysteries in a beautiful and memorable way. In that sense, all the passages we chose are mystagogical.

We have taken some liberties in editing the ancient texts for a modern audience. The Fathers of the Church were expansive preachers, and their congregations' attention spans had not been stunted by television, radio, or the Web. Many modern readers say they cannot process as much material as these ancient churchmen could preach. So we have condensed the material as much as we could without doing violence to the Fathers' spiritual message or their eloquence. Much of what we cut consisted of digressions on long-ago news and fashions, ancient cultural details that simply do not apply to the modern era, and the occasional personal quirks of the preacher. We eliminated, for example, St. Clement of Alexandria's lengthy speculation on the physiology of human milk production, as well as his ponderings on Christian vegetarianism. While these provide a fascinating glimpse of him as an individual, they do not reflect the essential teaching of the Church, and so they would be out of place in our course of mystagogy.

In the back of the book, we have listed sources where readers might find the full texts in good English translations. Some are accessible on the World Wide Web, as well as in readily available volumes.

Quotations from the Bible presented us with some difficulties. Some of the Fathers quoted from the earliest Greek Old Testament, called the Septuagint. The Septuagint differs at many points from the Hebrew texts used by most common modern translations. Later Fathers in the Western Church followed St. Jerome's Latin translation, called the Vulgate. And there were other Latin translations in circulation. Sometimes, it's impossible to say which version is at work in a particular homily — and the range of modern translations reflects the variety of ancient readings of the biblical text.

Thus, we have had to borrow from several different English translations. Most quotations in this book come from the *Revised Standard Version, Catholic Edition,* of the Bible. Sometimes, however, we have had to draw from others, and these are appropriately marked: the *New American Bible* (NAB); the *Confraternity of Christian Doctrine* (CCD); and the *Douay-Rheims* (DR).

CHAPTER 2

The Way to the Mysteries

For the first three hundred years of its existence, the Church faced intermittent, often brutal persecution. The practice of the faith was, in many places, strictly forbidden, punishable by torture and death. To become a Christian meant, at least, to take on social stigma and humiliation, but also, perhaps, to accept a shortened life, painfully ended.

Yet during that same period, the Church grew at a remarkable rate of forty percent per decade. The New Testament suggests that, by the end of the first century, there were a few thousand Christians in the world. In the early years of the fourth century, however, the Church could lay claim to the majority of people in the Roman Empire. Amid a population of sixty million, there were thirty-three million believers.

These were not thirty-three million "nominal" Christians or "Sunday Catholics." They could not be. These were Christians who, every day, had to lay down their life for the faith.

Why were so many people eager to take on such burdens and risks? Because they knew the reward was worth anything they could give in return, even to the last drop of their blood.

They had glimpsed the reward and tasted it, in the mysteries of God and in the sacraments of the Church.

Christian Initiation

In becoming a Christian, each seeker underwent a course of initiation. Its duration varied from place to place and from time to time. In some churches, the process lasted several years; in other places, only months. Sometimes, it depended upon the interior progress of the individual. Some lingered for a decade, while others raced forward.

The ancient process corresponded roughly to the four stages found today in the Rite of Christian Initiation for Adults (RCIA): inquiry, catechesis, purification, and initiation. During the inquiry phase, the seekers came forward with questions. If they agreed to become disciples, they would proceed to learn the faith from a preacher authorized by the Church. The disciples then strove to change their lives and their habits so that their thought, speech, and action conformed to the teaching of Jesus Christ.

These stages could be difficult and demanding, but the spiritual purification and enlightenment were ample rewards. Then as now, it was great to overcome destructive and hurtful habits, great to grow wiser and more moral. But in Christian life, purification and illumination are not the finish line. They are means to an end, and the end is union with God.

The sacraments, then, represent an "end" for the Christian. In baptism, we "become partakers of the divine nature" (2 Pet 1:4). We are "hid with Christ in God" (Col 3:3). In the

Eucharist, "our cup of blessing" is "a participation in the blood of Christ," and "the bread which we break" is a "participation in the body of Christ" (1 Cor 10:16).

For the Fathers of the Church, this was the meaning of salvation. This is what it meant to be saved: to share in the very life of God, to be made one with God. The early Christians boldly called this process "divinization" and "deification" — to "become divine," to be "made God."

St. Augustine said that in the sacraments, we become what we receive. After baptism, he said, "we have not only become Christians, but Christ himself.... Stand in awe and rejoice, we have become Christ!" Indeed, this divinization was the reason Christ established the sacraments. St. Clement of Alexandria wrote: "The Word of God became man so that you might learn from a man how a man may become God." And the learning was crucial, said St. Basil: "What is set before us is, as far as humanly possible, to be made like God. Without knowledge, though, we cannot be made like Him; and knowledge cannot be achieved without lessons."

The most important lessons came only with the end of the initiation process, after the new Christians had received the sacraments. It was then that they entered the phase of mystagogy.

These lessons were not what you might expect. They were not so much the transmission of facts or the memorization of a catechism (as important as these things were and are). They were, rather, the appropriation of a new worldview — a new way of understanding life on earth, life in heaven, and the meeting of the two in the sacraments of Jesus Christ.

Heaven meets earth in the sacraments. This is not mere wishful thinking or a metaphor taken too literally. It is something profoundly true and real. Less than a hundred years after the death of the last apostle, St. Irenaeus wrote: "Faith is established upon things truly real, so that we may believe what really is, as it is." The Fathers of the Church insisted on uncompromising realism in the belief of Christians. Yet it was not the realism of pagan materialists. It was not, it could not be, based on sensory data, on the mere perception of material things. For the sacraments represent divine mysteries, spiritual realities, and human senses cannot see them in their deepest reality.

Signs and Sacraments

What we see, said the Fathers, is a "sign" of an invisible reality. St. Augustine used the terms "sign" and "sacrament" interchangeably. This does not mean that the sacrament is merely a symbol. Nor does it mean that what we see is somehow more real than what's invisible. The sacrament is itself a reality, but one veiled, for now, in mystery. What the waters of baptism give is nothing less than birth into divine life. What we receive in the Eucharist is nothing less than the body, blood, soul, and divinity of Jesus Christ. These moments are as real on earth as they are in heaven; but only in heaven can anyone behold the mysteries in all their fullness, in all their glory.

Catechisms down through the ages have taught us that a sacrament is an outward sign established by Jesus Christ to give grace. But if it is a "sign," what does it signify? What does it stand for? St. Thomas Aquinas said there are many dimensions to the reality signified by the sacraments. "A sacrament," he said, "is a sign that commemorates what precedes it — Christ's Passion; demonstrates what is accomplished in us through Christ's Passion — grace; and prefigures what that Passion pledges to us — future glory" (see CCC, n. 1130).

The events of Israel's history, the events of Christ's life, and the consummation of history in glory are mystically represented, re-actualized, re-membered in the Church's liturgy. It is not just a nostalgic looking back. It is something really present. To God, there is no past, present, and future, just an eternal Now. When we partake in God's divine nature, as we do in the sacraments, we partake in all these mysteries, temporal and eternal. The historical events were indeed "once for all" (Heb 7:27), but the sacraments are the way that "all" enjoy a direct experience of that "once."

The *Catechism of the Catholic Church* puts this succinctly, drawing from a homily we include toward the end of this volume: "Jesus' words and actions during his hidden life and public ministry were already salvific, for they anticipated the power of his Paschal mystery. They announced and prepared what he was going to give the Church when all was accomplished. The mysteries of Christ's life are the foundations of what He would henceforth dispense in the sacraments, through the ministers of his Church, for 'what was visible in our Savior has passed over into his mysteries' " (n. 1115).

The Meaning of Everything

The lesson that mystagogy teaches us is nothing less than the meaning of the history of the world. What St. Paul called "the mystery hidden for ages" (Col 1:26) shows us God's patient instruction — how He built up, from the first moment of creation, a people worthy to understand the deepest truths of His plan. Only in the revelation of the New Covenant, with Jesus, the Word made flesh, do we understand the deeper meaning of all that Israel suffered in ancient history — all that God was trying to teach His children through the history of Israel.

This is what Christ taught His disciples, and what His disciples taught their disciples, in the Church's tradition: to read the Bible typologically, to see the events of the Old Testament as "a shadow of the good things to come" in Christ, and to see the events of the New Testament as a "true form" of realities that are eternal and invisible. The realities are present now in a way that they weren't before; but they're also veiled in a way that they won't be in heaven.

Mystagogical teaching continues the biblical and apostolic teaching in a very personal way, showing the newly baptized how they are to see their baptism, their individual salvation — as a singular event in that salvation history that began with the creation of the world. Mystagogy teaches the newborn Christian how to see the Church as the kingdom promised in the Old Covenant. Mystagogy teaches all of us that the sacraments are fulfillments of ancient promises and pledges of final fulfillment in the heavenly liturgy revealed in the last book of the Bible.

Mystagogy, according to the *Catechism,* "aims to initiate people into the mystery of Christ … by proceeding from the visible to the invisible, from the sign to the thing signified, from the 'sacraments' to the 'mysteries' " (n. 1075). Mystagogy shows us that, through the sacramental rites, sacred words actually do what they say they are doing: "I absolve you of your sins …" "This is my body …" We become participants in the New Covenant offered to humanity two thousand years ago in the death and resurrection of Jesus Christ.

Through mystagogy, we become bearers of the most secret wisdom, hidden from all those whom the world considers wise, but revealed to babies, who are newborn in Christ — newborn in baptism.

For only by the power of the sacraments can someone begin to perceive the sacraments as they are. Indeed, once people have been "divinized" by the sacraments, it is their right to be instructed about the sacraments, and it is the duty of the Church to give them that instruction.

To perceive the invisible, Christians need to learn a new kind of realism. That is what we learn in mystagogy. Mystagogy discloses both the signs and invisible realities.

Keeping Secrets

And, in the ancient Church especially, it was a real disclosure. For until the time of mystagogy, the new Christians had been forbidden to learn about the sacraments.

The "discipline of the secret" was the respectful silence the early Christians observed in regard to the mysteries of faith. When alluding to the sacraments in their homilies and commentaries, bishops and teachers would usually shift to a sort of code — a symbolic language dense with scriptural allusions, understandable only to someone living a deeply Christian life.

Almost everywhere the Fathers speak of the Eucharist, we find them urging their listeners not to repeat the doctrine to nonbelievers. Indeed, the unbaptized were forbidden to remain at the Mass beyond the Liturgy of the Word. The eucharistic prayer was for baptized Christians only. Why? In the year 197, the North African theologian Tertullian observed that "silence is due to the sacred mysteries" (*Apology* 7). His contemporary St. Clement of Alexandria confessed that he spoke in a cryptic way "so that the discovery of the sacred traditions may not be easy to any one of the uninitiated" (*Tapestries 7.18*).

In the mid-fourth century, St. Cyril of Jerusalem held nothing back as he wrote out his mystagogical lectures. Still, he sent his listeners home with a warning: "If a catechumen asks you what the teachers have said, tell him nothing. For we deliver you a mystery and a hope of the life to come. Guard the mystery for Him who gives the reward. Let none ever say to you, 'How will it harm you if I know?' So, too, the sick ask for wine; but if it is given at a wrong time, it causes delirium, and two evils arise: the sick man dies, and the physician is blamed" (*Catechetical Lectures,* Prologue 12).

Why did the Church keep the best of its Good News shrouded in secrecy? The Fathers offer many explanations:

- The mysteries of faith were so great that they should not be profaned by many words.
- The Church should not risk exposing the mysteries to ridicule by those who would not understand.
- Unbelievers had no right even to hear of the mysteries, because they had not received sufficient grace through baptism.
- The sacraments were intimate matters and, like intimacy in marriage, were not suitable subjects for public conversation.
- The best witness of eucharistic faith is not abundant words, but a pervasive culture of Christian charity. The third-century Didascalia put it eloquently: "Widows and orphans should be revered like the altar."

There was plenty of scriptural precedent for the discipline of the secret. Many of the Fathers cited the words of Jesus: "Do not give dogs what is holy; and do not throw your pearls before swine" (Mt 7:6). Our Lord did not mean to insult people who had never heard the Gospel. He was merely drawing an analogy that was certainly true: Unbelievers are not prepared to receive the mysteries; they wouldn't know what to do with them, any more than swine would know what to do with pearls.

The idea appears elsewhere in the Bible, and St. Basil traces the practice back to Moses himself, citing sound psychological reasons for keeping matters quiet: "Moses was wise enough to know that familiarity breeds contempt, while the unusual and unfamiliar naturally arouse a keen interest."

The pattern of secrecy and disclosure continued throughout the history of Israel. The first-century Jewish historian Josephus said that the Essenes — a monastic Jewish sect that some scholars connect with the origins of Christianity — would die rather than reveal the mysteries of faith to outsiders.

Indeed, the Jerusalem Temple can be seen as a stone-and-mortar model for mystagogy. In all of Israel, only one person, the high priest, was permitted beyond the curtain in the Temple's holy of holies. Only the children of the covenant, those initiated as Israelites (and later as Jews), were permitted in the Temple's inner court. But people of every nation were welcome to pray in the outer regions.

In a similar way, anyone, regardless of religion, might attend Mass up until the end of the Scripture readings; but only initiated Christians were permitted to stay for the mysteries. Only Christians could enter the holy of holies — that is, the mystery of the Eucharist, of Holy Communion — because only Christians had been baptized into the body of Christ the High Priest. The Church was "a royal priesthood, a holy nation" (1 Pet 2:9). Some scholars believe the Bible's Letter to the Hebrews served originally as a mystagogical text, precisely because it explains Christian initiation in terms of the Jerusalem Temple and the Christian sacraments: "Therefore, brethren, since we have confidence to enter the sanctuary by the blood of Jesus, by the new and living way which he opened for us through the curtain, that is, through his flesh, and since we have a great priest over the house of God, let us draw near with a true heart in full assurance of faith, with our hearts sprinkled clean from an evil conscience and our bodies washed with pure water" (Heb 10:19-22).

Into the Mysteries

In the last quarter-century, the word "mystagogy" has re-entered the Church's common vocabulary. The Church has made it the mandatory concluding phase of RCIA. The *Catechism of the Catholic Church* speaks warmly of mystagogy and puts it into practice. The *Catechism* even presents its own sacramental teaching in mystagogical form (see, for example, the mystagogy of baptism in nn. 1234-1245).

In fact, the *Catechism* seems to mandate that preaching and teaching help the faithful return to a mystagogical under-standing of the Christian life. Such preaching is the teaching of "the Lord ... and ... the Apostles and the Fathers of the Church." It "unveils what lay hidden under the letter of the Old Testament: the mystery of Christ." But it also must "help the faithful to open themselves to this spiritual under-standing of the economy of salvation as the Church's liturgy reveals it and enables us to live it" (CCC, nn. 1094-1095).

This is the point of mystagogy. Knowledge of the Bible isn't learning for learning's sake. Mystagogy enables us to live the sacred mysteries.

As Enrico Mazza, a modern scholar of the ancient Church, says, mystagogy is "the oral or written explanation of the mystery hidden in the Scriptures and celebrated in the liturgy." In liturgy, all time collapses to a point, and we participate in the events recorded and foretold in Scripture. But Scripture and liturgy are not just symbolic summaries of everything that has gone before us. Scripture and sacraments are themselves realities; but, at the same time, they are signs of something greater: an eternal mystery, fullness. Remember the words of St. Thomas Aquinas: The sacraments are "a pledge of future glory."

So the mysteries are more than past and present realities. They are a Reality of a higher order — a permanent abiding reality that we don't see just yet, except by faith. Theologians call this reality the supernatural order; the Bible calls it the "new creation" (2 Cor 5:17; Gal 6:15). For now, we walk by faith and not by sight.

The mystery is present here and now. But it's present only in the visible sacraments that point us to the invisible reality. The thing that we have to discover — the thing that mystagogy helps us to discover — is the truth and the reality of the supernatural order that originates in the Blessed Trinity. The seven sacraments are like the seven pillars on which wisdom builds her house (Prov 9:1). The sacraments are like pillars of the new house of God — the new creation, new heavens, new earth, new temple, new cosmos. We're living in God's new house right now, but we can't see it, can't smell it, can't hear it, can't taste it. We can't take a step from the natural order into the supernatural order, where the physical senses will not suffice. Death is the veil that hides the mysteries from us, but only for now, and only for our senses. For in the sacraments, we die with

Christ, we rise with Him, and we ascend with His glorified body, which has been enthroned on high. With Him, we pierce the veil, even now.

A Time of Grace

St. Leo the Great said that the days between Easter and Pentecost are God's favored time for revealing the mysteries. These were the days when Jesus Himself told His apostles what they previously could not bear; He told them about His sacraments. It's almost as if Mother Church has birthed us at Easter, and only now can we begin to take our first baby steps into a new world, a world more real, more permanent. It's less visible, certainly, but the things that are invisible are eternal and abiding: "We look not to the things that are seen but to the things that are unseen; for the things that are seen are transient, but the things that are unseen are eternal" (2 Cor 4:18).

These are exciting times, and you'll find that note of excitement in every one of the fifty meditations in this book. This is as it should be. In the fourth-century, a pilgrim from Spain witnessed the mystagogy in St. Cyril's church, and she wrote down what she saw for her friends at home: "While the bishop discusses and sets forth each point, the voices of those who applaud are so loud that they can be heard outside the church. And truly the mysteries are so unfolded that there is no one unmoved at the things that he hears to be so explained."

Imagine that: applause for the truths they had just discovered! Don't let yourself miss out on the excitement. Make an effort to pray, to meditate, to understand.

Think of how the technologies of recent centuries have enabled us to see life that was formerly invisible and unknowable in its details: The microscope showed us germs by the billion; the ultrasound showed us a tiny baby's earliest development in the womb. Well, now we know there is a Life we cannot perceive with our senses. We need to acquire and cultivate an interior sense of that Life — divine Life. We receive that sense by grace, through the sacraments, through contemplation, through mystagogy.

It's not that mystagogy is some kind of spiritual technique or technology. Rather, it is prayerful contemplation of the signs that lead us to the mysteries. Entering mystagogy is nothing less than allowing God to continue teaching us.

WEEK 1

with St. Basil the Great & St. Gregory of Nyssa

An Introduction
to the Mysteries

St. Basil the Great (330-379) and St. Gregory of Nyssa (335-395) were brothers, born to a noble family renowned for its scholarly achievement and deep holiness. Their paternal grandmother was revered as a saint; their maternal grandmother died as a martyr. Of the ten siblings in their family, three became bishops, and three are honored today as saints.

Christianity, however, is unlike nobility in many respects: Faith cannot be inherited, nor can it be transmitted through the genetic code. Neither Basil nor Gregory was particularly pious when each was young. Basil set his sights on an academic career, and he traveled from his native Pontus (in what is today Turkey) to the world's great schools for his studies. After years abroad in Athens and Constantinople, he returned home with awards and accomplishments, but a gnawing sense of emptiness inside. "I had wasted much time on foolishness," he wrote of his early years, "and I spent nearly all my youth in useless labors, devoted to the study of a wisdom that God had made foolish."

This was the moment of Basil's conversion. Most families at that time did not baptize their children as infants, so Basil presented himself for instruction in the faith and received the sacraments in due time. He discerned a vocation to the monastery and traveled to Egypt, Palestine, Syria, and Mesopotamia to observe the many ways men were living as monks.

Returning home again, he settled himself in seclusion on the banks of the Iris River. There he attracted many seekers and disciples, and soon he exercised a great influence over Christians in the region. His bishop asked him to become a priest, and Basil accepted. Basil would eventually be chosen as bishop of the great metropolis of Caesarea.

His brother Gregory, meanwhile, had married a woman named Theosebeia and begun work as a rhetorician. Gregory was a brilliant scholar, steeped in Greek philosophy, culture, and literature. Eventually, however, he and his wife decided to take the unusual step of living in celibacy within marriage and devoting themselves entirely to prayer and contemplation. Gregory grew in wisdom and wrote great works of theology and interpretation of the Bible. Eventually he, too, was called upon to be a bishop, though of a much smaller place, the little town of Nyssa.

History remembers Basil as a doer and Gregory as a thinker. Basil served tirelessly as a bishop, establishing hospitals, homeless shelters, and training centers for the unemployed. The charitable complex grew so large that the residents of Caesarea referred to it as a distinct city: "New Town."

As the leader of a major metropolitan church, Basil's influence extended through the entire world. The emperor once summoned him to court, only to find the invitation declined. Basil wrote voluminously, disciplined effectively, and fought successfully for the Catholic faith against many encroaching heresies.

Gregory was not as successful as an administrator. Indeed, even his brother Basil thought he was a weak leader. But Gregory was certainly the greater theologian. He wrote one of the Church's earliest systematic studies of doctrine. Some of his expositions on Scripture and prayer remain, even today, standard works in the field.

Basil and Gregory lived in a time of great doctrinal confusion and turmoil in the Church. Heresies abounded, entire dioceses were in open civil war, and discipline was difficult to carry out. While Basil was able to brush off the threats of a heretical emperor, Gregory was not as successful. The bishops of his region, who favored the heretics, tried Gregory on trumped-up charges of financial mismanagement. He was deposed, and for two years he wandered the countryside as a pilgrim and hermit until a new emperor restored him to office.

Basil never lived to see his fiftieth birthday. At his death, he was venerated as a saint and mourned by the whole city of Caesarea, both Christians and non-Christians.

Gregory helped to guide the universal Church through one of its most difficult periods. The Council of Constantinople convened in 381 to face the claims of heretics who denied the full divinity of Jesus Christ. He attended that council in the company of St. Cyril of Jerusalem, who is himself a featured Father in this book.

In his last years, Gregory was renowned for both his holiness and his brilliance. He died in 395.

In the passages that follow, Basil explains how the mysteries were preserved and transmitted by the apostles, in both oral and written forms. Gregory follows by examining the mysteries in light of Scripture and prayerful theological reflection.

1

~~~*~~~

St. Basil the Great

The Mystical Tradition

As a bishop, St. Basil was guardian and teacher of the Church's tradition, which was "passed on … in a mystery." The practices of prayer, the form and matter of the sacraments, the Sign of the Cross — these were treasures of doctrine kept hidden by the discipline of the secret. Yet they were more ancient even than the written Gospels. In the following passage from his treatise On the Holy Spirit, *written around the year 375, St. Basil distinguishes between "doctrine" and "proclamation." Doctrine, in his thought, includes the inner riches of the mystery, which can be understood only by those who have the grace of new life in baptism. Proclamation is the public and persuasive preaching of the Good News to all people. Proclamation, ideally, draws people toward doctrine.*

The Church preserves many beliefs and practices that are generally accepted or publicly commanded. Some are taken from written teaching; others have been passed on to us "in a mystery" by the tradition of the apostles. In relation to true religion, both of these have the same force. These no one will deny — no one, in any case, who is even moderately informed about the institutions of the Church. For if we were to try to reject any customs that have no written authority, on the ground that they are relatively unimportant, we would unintentionally injure the Gospel in its very vitals. Or, rather, we would make our public profession a mere formula and nothing more.

Let's take the first and most general example. Who has taught us — in writing — to make the Sign of the Cross over those who trust in the name of our Lord Jesus Christ? What writing has taught us to turn to the east when we pray? Which of the saints has left us in writing the words of the invocation at the revelation of the bread of the Eucharist and the cup of blessing? No, it's well known that we are not content with what the apostle or the Gospel has recorded, but both in preface and conclusion we add other words because they are important to the validity of the ministry, and these we derive from unwritten teaching.

What's more, we bless the water of baptism and the oil of the chrism, and besides this the catechumen who is being baptized. On what written authority do we do this? Isn't our authority the silent and mystical tradition? By what written word is the anointing of oil itself taught? And whence comes the custom of washing three times in baptism? And what about the other customs of baptism? From what Scripture do we derive the renunciation of Satan and his angels?

Doesn't this come from that private and secret teaching that our fathers guarded in silence, out of the reach of nosy meddling and curious investigation? They had learned their lesson well: The awesome dignity of the mysteries is best preserved by silence. What the uninitiated are not even allowed to look at was hardly likely to be publicly paraded about in written documents.

Why didn't mighty Moses open all the parts of the tabernacle to everyone? The profane he stationed outside the sacred barriers. The first courts he conceded to those who were more pure. But he judged only the Levites worthy of being servants of God. Sacrifices, burnt offerings, and the rest of the priestly work he assigned to the priests. And from all these people, he chose only one to be admitted to the shrine — and even this one not always, but on only one day in the year — and on that one day there was an appointed time for his entry, so that he might gaze on the Holy of Holies amazed at the strangeness and novelty of the sight.

Moses was wise enough to know that familiarity breeds contempt, while the unusual and unfamiliar naturally arouse a keen interest. In the same way, the apostles and Fathers who first laid down laws for the Church guarded the awesome dignity of the mysteries in the discipline of secrecy and silence. After all, what is repeated abroad at random among common folk is no mystery at all.

This is the reason for our tradition of unwritten precepts and practices: that the knowledge of our doctrines may not become overly familiar and so neglected and held in contempt by the crowd.

Doctrine and proclamation are two distinct things. The former is kept in silence; the latter is proclaimed to all the world. One form of this silence is the obscurity used in Scripture, which makes the meaning of doctrine difficult to understand for the reader. We all look to the east at our prayers, but few of us know that we are seeking our own old country, Paradise, which God planted in Eden in the east (Gen 2:8). We pray standing on Sunday, but we do not all know the reason. On the day of the resurrection [in Greek, the word is literally "standing again"] we stand up in order to remind ourselves of the grace given to us — not only because we rose with Christ, and are bound to "seek the things that are above" (Col 3:1), but also because the day seems to be in some sense an image of the time we await — the age that follows this present time, the day that knows no evening or night, the day that never ends or grows old. The Church teaches her foster children, then, to offer their Sunday prayers while standing, as a continual reminder of the endless life, so that we may not neglect to plan to arrive there.

Time will fail me if I try to tell all the unwritten mysteries of the Church.

Take It to Prayer

Doctrine and proclamation are two distinct things. The former is kept in silence; the latter is proclaimed to all the world.

If we try to reject Church customs that have no written authority, we injure the Gospel.

Familiarity breeds contempt, while the unusual and unfamiliar naturally arouse a keen interest.

Learn It by Heart

The awesome dignity of the mysteries is best preserved by silence.

Apply It to Your Life

Strive to keep a sense of reverence and awe before God's mysteries.

2

St. Gregory of Nyssa

On the Power of Ordinary Things

The following passage comes from St. Gregory's sermon on the feast of Epiphany, probably in the year 383. On that day, the ancient Church commemorated the many manifestations of Jesus' divinity, most especially His anointing with the Holy Spirit at His baptism in the Jordan River. St. Gregory urges us to learn that our baptism — indeed, every sacrament we receive — is a close encounter with God and a sharing in God's divine nature. This is a profound statement of the Church's teaching on the sacraments, and its deep roots in both the Old and New Testaments. Very ordinary materials — water, oil, bread, wine, wood, and stone — now, with the words of blessing, become holy things for a holy people and signs of deeper mysteries. St. Gregory opens the eyes of our souls to the supernatural dimension of all Christian liturgy.

Do not dismiss the divine washing. Don't think of it as something common because it uses mere water. For the power at work is mighty, and wonderful are the things that work by that power.

This holy altar, by which I stand, is made of stone, ordinary in its nature, no different from the other slabs of stone that build our houses and line our pavements. But it was consecrated to the service of God. It received the blessing. Now it is a holy table, an altar undefiled, no longer touched by everyone's hands, but only by the priest's, and even then only with reverence.

The bread, too, is at first common bread. But when the sacramental action consecrates it, it is called the Body of Christ, for it becomes the Body of Christ.

So with the sacramental oil; so with the wine. Before the blessing, they are worth little. But afterward they are made holy by the Spirit.

The same power of the Word makes the priest worthy of veneration and honor. The new blessing separates him from his common life with the people. Yesterday he was one of the crowd, one of the people. Now, suddenly, he has become a guide, a leader, a teacher of righteousness, an instructor in hidden mysteries. And this he does without any change in body or form. But, while he appears to be the man he was before, his invisible soul has really been transformed to a higher condition by some invisible power and grace.

There are many things that appear to be contemptible, but accomplish mighty works. This is especially true when you search the ancient history. Moses' rod was a hazel switch — common wood that any hands might cut and carry, and use as they please before tossing it into the fire. But when God wanted to work miracles through that rod — great miracles, beyond the power of words to express — the wood was changed into a serpent. Another time, he struck the water, and he turned the water into blood; then he called forth a countless brood of frogs; then he divided the sea, cut to its depths without flowing together again (see Ex 4-14).

Likewise, the mantle of one of the prophets, a simple goatskin, made Elisha famous throughout the whole world (see 2 Kings 2:8).

The wood of the cross holds saving power for everyone, even though it is, I'm told, a piece of a common tree of little value.

A bramble bush showed the presence of God to Moses (see Ex 3:2).

The remains of Elisha raised a dead man to life (see 2 Kings 13:21).

Clay gave sight to a man who was blind from the womb (see Jn 9:6).

All these, though they were material things without soul or sense, were made instruments for the working of miracles when they received the power from God.

In the same way, water, though it is nothing but water, renews someone to spiritual rebirth, when the grace from above makes it holy.

Take It to Prayer

Material things, without soul or sense, are made instruments for the working of miracles when they receive the power from God.

Many things appear to be contemptible, but accomplish mighty works.

Common bread, blessed by the sacramental action, is called the Body of Christ, for it becomes the Body of Christ.

Learn It by Heart

The wood of the cross holds saving power for everyone, even though it is a piece of a common tree of little value.

Apply It to Your Life

Give careful attention to the gestures, symbols, and objects used in the Mass and other traditional prayers. Pray about them and learn what they mean. Reject the notion that such things could ever be reduced to mere ritual.

3

St. Gregory of Nyssa

Through the Maze of Life

St. Gregory borrows a term from the Letter to the Hebrews and shows us Jesus Christ as the "pioneer of our salvation." Without Christ, we were like children lost in a maze, or inmates locked away in a prison of death, with no exit. But in becoming a man, God blazed a trail for us to follow. He knew the limitations of our human nature, that we could not produce "an exact and entire imitation" of our divine Pioneer. So He gave us the sacraments and endowed them with His own divine power over life and death. This passage comes from St. Gregory's Great Catechism, *which he wrote as a training manual for Christian teachers around the year 385.*

The descent into the water, with the threefold immersion, involves a mystery. For the means of our salvation received its power not so much from the words Christ taught as from the deeds He did. Christ has accomplished an actual fellowship with man, and He has given life as a living fact. In taking on human flesh, He made human flesh divine. And in order that everything related to that flesh may be saved, it was necessary that something in the baptismal process should produce a kind of resemblance between those who follow and Him who leads the way.

It is, in fact, impossible for people to reach the same goal unless they travel by the same routes. People lost in the corridors of mazes can navigate the twists and turns and blind alleys if they happen to find someone who has been through it all before. They can get to the end by following behind — which they could not do if they did not follow their leader step by step. So I beg you to listen: Our human minds cannot thread the maze of this life unless we pursue that same path as He did. He was once in it, yet He got beyond the difficulties that hemmed Him in. By the maze I mean that prison of death that leaves no exit and encloses the miserable human race.

What, then, have we seen in the case of the Pioneer of our salvation (see Heb 2:10, 12:2)? Three days of death and then life again. Now there must be some sort of plan to make us resemble Him in these things. What, then, is that plan? Everything that dies finds its proper and natural place in the earth in which it is laid and hidden. Now earth and water have much in common. Alone of the elements they have weight and gravitate downward; they live in each other; they confine each other.

Since in death the Author of life was subject to burial in the earth, in keeping with our common nature, we imitate that death in the next-closest element.

He, the Man from above, took death upon Himself. He was buried in the earth, and He returned back to life on the third day. So everyone who is joined to Him by virtue of His body may look forward to the same happy ending — I mean, he may arrive at life by having water, instead of earth, poured over him. Submerged in that element three times represents for him the three-days-delayed grace of the resurrection.

Nature does not allow us an exact and entire imitation, but it receives now as much as it can receive, while it keeps the rest for a later time. What, then, is the extent of our imitation? It consists in suppressing our sins in the sign of death that's given by water. Sin is not completely wiped away, but there is a kind of break in the continuity of evil. By our penance and by our imitation of death, we are freed from the innate tendency to evil; by penance we move ahead to a hatred of sin, and by the death we suppress evil. We imitate the transcendent power as far as our poor nature can, by having the water three times poured on us and rising again from the water. Thus we enact that saving burial and resurrection that took place on the third day.

Keep in mind: We have the power to be in the water and to rise out of it. He who has the universe at His disposal immersed Himself in death — as we immersed ourselves in the water — to return to His own blessedness. Each in proportion to the measure of his natural power achieved the results that were within reach. A human being may touch the water and yet be safe. The divine power, with infinitely greater ease, can handle death, and even be immersed in it, and yet not be changed or injured by it.

Notice, then, that we need to rehearse beforehand in the water the grace of our resurrection. We must come to learn that, as far as easiness goes, it's the same thing for us to be baptized with water and to rise again from death.

Take It to Prayer

By penance we move forward to a hatred of sin.

We imitate God's power, as far as our poor nature can, by having water poured over us and by rising again from the water. We rehearse in water the grace of our resurrection.

There is an inseparable bond between baptism with water and rising again from death.

Learn It by Heart

In taking on human flesh, Christ made human flesh a powerful instrument of the divine.

Apply It to Your Life

Give thanks daily for the gift you received in baptism.

4

St. Gregory of Nyssa

Passing Sinless Through the Sea

In the story of the Israelites' escape from Egypt, St. Gregory found many lessons for growth in the spiritual life. Following St. Paul, he saw the passage through the Red Sea as a foreshadowing of baptism (1 Cor 10:1-2). We pass through the waters as the Israelites passed through the Red Sea (Ex 14). As they left behind slavery in Egypt, so we leave behind our slavery to sin. This spiritual interpretation of Scripture comes from St. Gregory's Life of Moses, *which many people consider the masterpiece of his mystical works. He wrote it around 390-392, toward the end of his life.*

We escape the Egyptian army only to grow terrified by new assaults of temptation beyond the borders. Every time, however, our guide arrives with unexpected help from above. And whenever the enemy with his army pursues us as we flee, the sea is forced to let us pass. At this passage, the guide was the cloud; and our ancestors have used this name to refer to the grace of the Spirit; for He guides the righteous toward salvation. Whoever follows Him will pass through the water. He will clear a way for him and bring sure redemption, drowning in the sea anyone who would pursue us to enslave us.

Pay attention, and you will understand the mystery of the water into which we descend with the entire enemy army and emerge alone, our enemies drowned in the sea. Everyone knows that the Egyptian army represents the enslaving passions of the human soul: They are the horses, chariots, and charioteers, the soldiers armed with bows, slings, and heavier artillery, and all the rest of the enemy forces. How is that army different from our tendencies to anger, our sensuality, despair, and greed? They rush into the water after the Israelites, their prey. But under the guidance of the enlightening cloud, the water gives life to those who take refuge in it, but deals death to those who pursue.

Holy Scripture teaches that those who pass through the water must emerge with nothing from the enemy's army. For if they emerge with the enemy, they will remain in slavery even after the waters, for they will have dragged out the tyrant who should have drowned in the sea. The meaning is this: All those who pass through the mystical waters of baptism must drown the whole array of sins that attack them, whether in thought or in deed — greed, lust, vanity, pride, anger, rage, jealousy, envy, and such — for these are the passions that come naturally to our human nature. In this story we are commanded to drown every form of sin in the saving waters of baptism, and then come up from the waters alone.

After crossing the sea, the Israelites encamped in a place where the water was bitter and undrinkable (Ex 15:23). But into that water Moses threw wood, which made it a sweet drink to quench their thirst. The text matches our experience:

When we give up the "Egyptian" pleasures that had enslaved us before the passage through the water, life at first seems bitter and difficult. We miss our former pleasures. But once the wood hits the water — that is, once we unite ourselves to the mystery of the resurrection, which began with the wood of the cross — then the virtuous life grows sweeter and more refreshing than any sensual pleasure, because this new life is sweetened by our hope in the things to come.

Take It to Prayer

All those who pass through the mystical waters of baptism must drown the whole array of sins that attack them in thought or in deed.

We are commanded to drown every form of sin in the saving waters of baptism, and then come up from the waters alone.

When we give up sinful pleasures, life at first seems bitter. But once we unite ourselves to the mystery of the cross, then the virtuous life grows sweeter.

Learn It by Heart

The water gives life to those who take refuge in it, but deals death to the sins that pursue.

Apply It to Your Life

Make a list of any sinful habits that remain in you after your passage through the "mystical waters." Make a plan for overcoming them with God's help.

5

St. Gregory of Nyssa

Actions Speak Louder Than Words

Through baptism we share in God's life. But through our every-day actions we must grow in that life, freely respond to the gift of grace, and come ever more to resemble our Father, God. Here we encounter a recurring theme in the baptismal teachings of the Fathers: Divinization is a gift fully and freely given by God, but it requires our full and free acceptance. If we share His nature, we will imitate His actions.

All you who are gladdened by the gift of rebirth, all you who boast of that saving renewal, show me, after the sacramental grace, the resulting change in your ways.

Let the purity of your life show what a difference your conversion has made. For nothing visible has been changed. Your body looks the same, and the cast of visible nature is no different. But there surely must be some outward proof by which we may recognize the newborn person, something that clearly sets the new apart from the old.

And these, I think, are to be found in the deeds of the soul, the actions by which the soul removes itself from its old, customary life and enters into a newer way of life. Such a soul can and will clearly teach its acquaintances that it has become something different from what it was. It will be unrecognizable as its old self.

If you believe me and keep my words as a law, you'll find that this is the way of change. If someone before baptism was immoral, covetous, grasping at the goods of others, a heckler, a liar, a slanderer — and all that goes along with these things, and all that flows from them — then let him now become orderly, sober, content with his own possessions, willing to share with the poor, truthful, courteous, affable — in a word, following every praiseworthy course of conduct.

As darkness is dispelled by light, so the old nature disappears when clothed with the works of righteousness. Notice how Zacchaeus, after the change of his life, put to death the tax collector that he was, made fourfold restitution to those whom he had unjustly damaged, and the rest he divided with the poor — the treasure that he had extorted from the poor (Lk 19:1-10). The evangelist Matthew, a tax collector like Zacchaeus, after his call changed his life as if it had been a mask. Paul was a persecutor, but after the grace given to him he became an apostle, bearing the weight of his chains for Christ's sake.

So you should be in your rebirth. So you should blot out your habits that lead you to sin. Just so the sons of God should live, because after the grace He has given us, we are called His children. And so we need to carefully study our Father's characteristics, so that by fashioning and framing ourselves to the likeness of our Father, we may seem true children of Him who calls us to adoption through grace.

Take It to Prayer

～✲～

You who boast of that saving renewal, show others the resulting change in your ways.

As darkness is dispelled by light, so the old nature disappears when clothed with the works of righteousness.

We need to study the characteristics of our Father God, and to grow in His likeness, so that we may seem His true children.

Learn It by Heart

～✲～

Let the purity of your life show what a difference your conversion has made.

Apply It to Your Life

～✲～

Put yourself in the place of others: your family, friends, neighbors, and co-workers. How do they see your likeness to God? How might you come to better resemble your heavenly Father?

6

St. Gregory of Nyssa

Choosing to Be Born

As humans we suffer from age, corruption, uncertainty, betrayal, inner turmoil, and the fickle whims of other people. Things change, often for the worse, and this change marks a gradual dying. We are born into this anxious life. But what if we could choose another birth — one as true, unchanging, and undying as God Himself?

All other things that are born are subject to the impulse of those who beget them. Only the spiritual birth depends on the power of the person being born.

Seeing that the choice is free, it would be good for those who wish to be begotten to find out what kind of father would be best for them, and what element should make up their nature.

Again, it is in the power of such children to choose their parents. Since, then, there are two kinds of existence, created and uncreated; and since the uncreated world remains unchanged and unmoved, while the created is subject to change and alteration; of which should they prefer to be the offspring? Of something that is always changing, or something whose nature is changeless, steadfast, consistent, and unvarying in goodness?

The Gospel gives us three Persons and names through whom the birth of believers takes place, and anyone who is begotten by this Trinity is equally begotten of the Father, and of the Son, and of the Holy Spirit. For the Gospel says: "that which is born of the Spirit is spirit" (Jn 3:6), and it is "in Christ" that Paul begets, and the Father is the "father of all" (Rom 4:11).

So let the mind be clear as it makes its choice, lest it make itself the child of some fickle nature, when it can make the steady and unchanging nature the founder of its life. Those who confess that the Holy Trinity is uncreated enter on the steady, unchanging life. For those who are born must be related to their begetter.

Which, then, offers the greater advantage: to enter the unchangeable life, or to be tossed about by the waves of a lifetime of uncertainty and change?

Take It to Prayer

Only the spiritual birth — the birth of baptism — depends on the power of the person being born.

Anyone begotten by the Trinity is equally begotten of the Father, and of the Son, and of the Holy Spirit.

Which offers the greater advantage: to enter the unchangeable life, or to be tossed about in a lifetime of uncertainty and change?

Learn It by Heart

～⋙⋘～

Only in the spiritual life are children free to choose their parents.

Apply It to Your Life

～⋙⋘～

Take a brief moment, many times a day, to call on God silently as "Father!" Place a discreet reminder at your workstation, by your phone, on your desk — wherever you'll see it often.

7

St. Gregory of Nyssa

The Light That Lifts Us Up

Eustathia, Ambrosia, and Basilissa were three women who had consecrated their lives to God. St. Gregory wrote to give them advice and encouragement in the ways of prayer. In one brief passage, he sums up the difference God made by becoming human. He enlightened our lives. He made us divine. This is what it means to be saved.

When the sun plunges his beam into the gloom, he doesn't dim the beam's brightness. Instead, the beam changes the darkness into light. So also the true Light, shining in our gloom, was not overshadowed, but rather enlightened the gloom by means of itself.

Our humanity was in darkness. As Scripture says: "They have neither knowledge nor understanding, they walk about in darkness" (Ps 82:5). Then the Illuminator of this darkened world darted the beam of His divinity through our whole composite nature, through both soul and body, and so He took all humanity by means of His own light, and He lifted it up and made it just what He is Himself. This divinity was not made perishable, though it inhabited a perishable body, so neither was it changed, though it healed all that was changeful in our soul.

Take It to Prayer

The true Light, shining in our gloom, was not overshadowed. He enlightened the gloom.

The Light darted the beam of His divinity through our soul and body, and so He took all humanity by means of His own light.

When God became man, divinity was not changed, though it healed all that was changeful in our soul.

Learn It by Heart

He took all humanity and lifted it up, and He made it just what He is Himself.

Apply It to Your Life

Ask yourself: Do I extend the divine light of Christ in the places where I live and work? Am I a voice of hope or a voice of gloom?

WEEK 2

with St. Cyril of Jerusalem

On Baptism and Confirmation

St. Cyril of Jerusalem (315-386) had the difficult privilege of living a long life in interesting times. A contemporary of Sts. Basil and Gregory, he faced many of the same heresies in his diocese, as well as the same sort of political intrigue. Like Gregory, he fell victim to the intrigue; only in Cyril's case, it happened not once, but three times.

Cyril was ordained to the priesthood when he was around the age of thirty, and within three years he was elevated to bishop of Jerusalem. Jerusalem was honored for its historical importance; it was a popular place of pilgrimage, but it was no longer the center of scholarship and commerce that it had once been.

At the time, the Church of that region was divided between those who believed Jesus was "true God from true God," and those who believed he was merely a semi-divine creature of God. This latter group was known as the Arians, after Arius, the founder of the heresy.

The man who consecrated Cyril as bishop was an Arian, and so Cyril carried that taint with him. Some of his opponents, who were faithful Catholics, accused him of befriending heretics. If Cyril did try to befriend heretics, perhaps it was to convert them. In any event, the heretics repaid any supposed friendship with pointed hostility. They had him expelled from Jerusalem precisely because he preached the doctrine of Christ as the Church had defined it at the Council of Nicea.

Cyril's life as a bishop was filled with hardship. Of his thirty-five years in that role, sixteen were spent in exile from his diocese. First, the Arians drove him out, then the pagan emperor, then an Arian emperor.

The suspicion of heresy lingered about him until he was examined and vindicated by his friend St. Gregory of Nyssa, who was at that time among the most revered theologians in the world.

We actually know little else about Cyril, except that he attended the Church's councils and synods. He was a great promoter of the faith at the Council of Constantinople in 381.

The writings that have secured his reputation in history — and the honorific title of Doctor of the Church — are his twenty-four *Catechetical Lectures*. Eighteen of these are addressed to candidates awaiting baptism. Cyril himself gives the date of those as 347, when he was still a priest. The remaining lectures are mystagogical, delivered to newly baptized Christians. Some scholars believe that St. Cyril's mystagogical lectures were delivered at a much later date, perhaps decades later, than the earlier group. We have no way of knowing. Both sets of lectures were given at Jerusalem's Church of the Holy Sepulcher, built at the site of Jesus' tomb.

The portions included in this book deal with baptism and confirmation (also called "chrismation," for the anointing with chrism). In the Eastern churches, then as now, these two sacraments were usually administered together. The *Catechism of the Catholic Church* says the sacrament of confirmation is necessary "for the completion of baptismal grace" (n. 1285). This echoes the testimonies of the early Church, where chrismation is often called the baptism of the Spirit. In St. Cyril's own lifetime, the Council of Laodicea proclaimed: "Those who are baptized must after baptism be anointed with the heavenly chrism, and be partakers of the kingdom of Christ."

St. Cyril's lectures give us a vivid description of the rites as they were performed by the saint himself. Moreover, they tell us something about the saint. The tone of St. Cyril's lectures is steady, serene, joyful, poetic. Despite the treachery, he never grew cynical about human nature — or divine nature. He never lost his sense of awe.

Cyril died in 386.

8

St. Cyril of Jerusalem

Turn from the Old to the New

St. Cyril is speaking to the newly baptized immediately after their baptism. Step by step, he guides them through the ritual they have just experienced. But, more importantly, he takes them beyond the ritual to the unseen realities that it signifies. He evokes many events from the Old Testament, but not merely as actions of the past. St. Cyril moves his hearers "from the old to the new, from the figure to the reality." He shows his listeners — and us readers — that we are all midstream in salvation history, caught up in its current. Those long-ago events transpired for our sake. St. Cyril reveals the invisible, but he never loses touch with the sights, sounds, and smells of ordinary life. He helps his hearers to identify the near occasions of sins in their workaday world. He savages the entertainment industry of his day for its explicit violence and unchastity.

I have long wished, O true and beloved children of the Church, to speak to you about these spiritual and heavenly mysteries. But since I knew that seeing is far more persuasive than hearing, I waited till now, when your present experience has left you more open to the influence of my words. Now I might lead you by the hand into the brighter and more fragrant meadow of the paradise before us.

You were found worthy of divine and life-giving baptism, and now you are ready to receive the more sacred mysteries. Now it's time to set before you a banquet of more perfect instructions. So let us teach you these things exactly, that you may know the effect worked upon you on that evening of your baptism.

First you entered into the vestibule of the baptistery. There, facing west, you heard the command to stretch forth your hand, and, as if you were in the presence of Satan, you renounced him. Now you must know that this was prefigured in ancient history. For when Pharaoh, that most bitter and cruel tyrant, was oppressing the free and noble Hebrews, God sent Moses to bring them out of the evil bondage of the Egyptians. Then the doorposts were anointed with the blood of a lamb, that the destroyer might flee from the houses that had the sign of the blood; and the Hebrew people were marvelously delivered. But, after their rescue, the enemy pursued them, and saw the sea miraculously parted for them. Nevertheless he went on, following close in their footsteps, and was all at once overwhelmed and engulfed in the Red Sea.

Now turn from the old to the new, from the figure to the reality. There we have Moses sent from God to Egypt. Here, we have Christ sent forth from His Father into the world. There, so that Moses might lead forth an afflicted people out of Egypt. Here, so that Christ might rescue those who are oppressed in the world under sin. There, the blood of a lamb was the spell against the destroyer. Here, the blood of the Lamb without blemish, Jesus Christ, is made the charm to scare evil spirits. There, the tyrant was pursuing that ancient people all the way to the sea. And here, the daring and shameless spirit, the author of evil, follows you even to the streams of salvation. The tyrant of old was drowned in the sea; and this present one disappears in the water of salvation.

Nevertheless, you are asked to say, with arm outstretched toward him as if he were present, "I renounce you, Satan." I wish also to give the reason why you stand facing west; for you need to know. The west is the direction from which we see darkness coming, and the devil is darkness and reigns in darkness. That is why, looking symbolically toward the west, you renounce that dark and gloomy tyrant.

What, then, did each of you stand up and say? "I renounce you, Satan" — I renounce you, you wicked and most cruel tyrant! And your words meant: "I fear your power no longer; for Christ has overthrown it, having shared with me in flesh and blood. He died to destroy death, that I might not be enslaved forever."

"I renounce you" — you crafty and most subtle serpent. "I renounce you" — schemer that you are, who under the pretense of friendship contrived all disobedience, and brought our first parents to rebel against God. "I renounce you, Satan" — the maker and promoter of all wickedness.

Then, in a second phrase, you are taught to say, "and all your works." The works of Satan are all sin, and this, too, you must renounce — just as someone who has escaped a tyrant has surely escaped his weapons as well. All sin, therefore, of every kind, is included in the works of the devil. You can be sure of this: that all you say, especially at that most thrilling hour, is written in God's books; so when you do anything contrary to these promises, you shall be judged as a transgressor. You renounce the works of Satan; that is, all deeds and thoughts that are contrary to reason.

Then you say: "And all his pomps." Now the pomp of the devil is the madness of theaters, and horse races, and the circus, and all such worthlessness. From these, the holy man prays to be delivered, saying to God, "Turn my eyes from looking at vanities" (Ps 119:37). Don't be interested in the madness of the theater, where you would see the obscene antics of the actors, the mockeries and rudeness, and the frantic dancing of perverts. Nor should you be interested in the madness of the wild-beast hunts in the circus. They pamper their bellies with meats and, in the process, risk becoming meat in the belly of wild beasts. It's fair to say that their belly is their god (see Phil 3:19), and, in serving him, they cast away their life in the arena. Shun horse races, too, those frantic and soul-destroying spectacles. For all these are the pomp of the devil.

Take It to Prayer

You were found worthy of divine and life-giving baptism, and now you are ready to receive the more sacred mysteries. Now it's time to set before you a banquet of more perfect instructions.

"I renounce you, Satan" — you crafty and most subtle serpent — who under the pretense of friendship, brought our first parents to rebel against God.

All you say, especially at that most thrilling hour, is written in God's books; so when you do anything contrary to these promises, you shall be judged as a transgressor.

Learn It by Heart

Pharaoh, the tyrant of old, was drowned in the sea; and Satan, this present one, disappears in the water of salvation.

Apply It to Your Life

Consider your pastimes in light of your new life. Are the movies and television shows you watch, the books and magazines you read, suitable for a child of God?

9

St. Cyril of Jerusalem

Don't Look Back

Spiritual masters have always spoken of the Christian life as "combat." St. Cyril makes it clear that this is not a mere metaphor. The enemy is real, and he fights with the power of an angelic intelligence, but even that is powerless before Jesus Christ. Still, Satan will try to win back what he has lost. He will try to turn our attention to the pleasures we enjoyed in our former life. St. Cyril shows that it is not pleasure, but pain, that awaits us if we turn back to "what lies behind."

If, after renouncing Satan and associating yourself with Christ, you fall under the influence of demons, you'll find the tyrant more bitter. Before, perhaps, he treated you as his own, and went easy on you; but now he has been exasperated by you. So you would suffer the loss of Christ, and experience Satan's tyranny.

Haven't you heard the old story of Lot and his daughters? He was saved with his daughters, when he had gained the mountain, while his wife became a pillar of salt, set up as a monument forever, in memory of her wicked choice — her turning back. Be careful, then; never to turn back to "what lies behind" (Phil 3:13). You've put your hand to the plow;

don't turn back to the bitter taste of the things of this world (see Lk 9:62). Escape to the mountain, instead, to Jesus Christ, that stone cut by no human hands (see Dan 2:45), that has filled the world.

When you renounce Satan, you utterly break your covenant with him, that ancient treaty with hell (see Is 28:15). At once you find open God's paradise, which He planted towards the east. It is from there that our first father was banished for his sins. Your turning from west to east, the place of lights, was a symbol of this. Then you were told to say, "I believe in the Father, and in the Son, and in the Holy Spirit, and in one baptism of repentance."

Fortified by this creed, then, "Be sober, be watchful." For "your adversary the devil prowls around like a roaring lion, seeking someone to devour" (1 Pet 5:8). But while, in the past, death was mighty and devoured, at the holy bath of regeneration God has wiped away tears from all faces (see Is 25:8). For you shall mourn no longer, now that you have put off the old nature (see Eph 4:22); but you shall keep the holy day, clothed in the garment of salvation, which is Jesus Christ.

Take It to Prayer

"Your adversary the devil prowls around like a roaring lion, seeking someone to devour" (1 Pet 5:8).

When you renounce Satan, you utterly break your covenant with him, that ancient treaty with hell.

Associating with Christ, you have exasperated Satan.

Learn It by Heart

You've put your hand to the plow, don't turn back to the bitter things of this world

Apply It to Your Life

Satan works evil with tremendous power, but he cannot harm us as long as we remain with Christ. Silently pray the name of Jesus many times today.

10

St. Cyril of Jerusalem

Naked and Unashamed

The baptized person is a new creation, like Adam and Eve in the garden, naked and unashamed. In St. Cyril's time, one stripped oneself completely before being anointed with oil from head to toe. In the ancient world, oil was a staple in the diet and the most common medicine. Thus it was a symbol of strength and power. Priests were anointed when ordained to their office, as were kings when they ascended the throne. St. Cyril shows that the Christian's true power is the imitation of Christ in His weakness, stripped and bound to the cross. St. Cyril takes these images of nakedness — powerless and shameful in the eyes of the world — and invests them with the power of the nakedness of bride and groom. The newly baptized speak timeless words of love, with the voice of the Church, which is the Spouse of Christ, naked and unashamed.

As soon as you entered the baptistery, you put off your garment. This was a sign that you had "put off the old nature with its practices" (Col 3:9). You stripped yourselves in imitation of Christ, who was stripped naked on the cross. By His nakedness He put off from Himself the principalities and powers, and openly triumphed over them on the tree. And since the enemy powers had once made their home in

your members, you may no longer wear that old garment —
I do not at all mean the clothes you can see, but the "old
nature which … is corrupt through deceitful lusts" (Eph
4:22). Once you have put off that nature, never again put it
on, but say with the Spouse of Christ in the Song of Songs,
"I had put off my garment, how could I put it on?" (Sgs 5:3).
What a marvel! You were naked in the sight of all, and you
were not ashamed. For truly you bore the likeness of the
first-formed Adam, who was naked in the garden and was not
ashamed (see Gen 2:25).

Then, when you were stripped, you were anointed with
the oil of exorcism, from the very hairs of your head to your
feet, and you were made partakers of the good olive tree,
Jesus Christ. For you were cut off from the wild olive tree and
grafted onto the good one, and were made to share the richness of the true olive tree (see Rom 11:17-24). The oil of
exorcism, therefore, was a symbol of the sharing in the richness of Christ. It is a token to drive away every trace of hostile influence. Just as the breath of the saints and the
invocation of God's name scorch like the fiercest flame and
drive out devils, so too, this oil of exorcism receives such
power by the invocation of God and by prayer, as not only
to burn and cleanse away the traces of sins, but also to chase
away all the invisible powers of the devil.

Take It to Prayer

You stripped yourselves in imitation of Christ on the cross. By His nakedness He put off from Himself the enemy powers, and openly triumphed over them.

At your baptism, you bore the likeness of the first-formed Adam, who was naked in the garden and was not ashamed.

The breath of the saints, the invocation of God's name, and the exorcised oil burn and cleanse away the traces of sins, and chase away all the invisible powers of the devil.

Learn It by Heart

The oil of exorcism was a symbol of the sharing in the richness of Christ.

Apply It to Your Life

God's constant presence is a comfort to those who are free from sin. Resolve to break free of any habitual sins, so that you may stand before Him unashamed.

11

~ع୨~

St. Cyril of Jerusalem

Remain in Light

When St. Cyril compared the immersion of baptism to the laying of Christ in the tomb, his words carried a special poignancy. For he preached before the very tomb of Christ as he called baptism "the sacramental sign of Christ's suffering." In baptism, we do not suffer, and yet we share mystically in the sufferings of Jesus.

After that, you were led to the holy pool of divine baptism, as Christ was carried from the cross to the tomb. And each of you was asked whether you believed in the name of the Father, and of the Son, and of the Holy Spirit, and you made that saving profession, and descended three times into the water, and you ascended again. This also suggests symbolically Christ's three days of burial. As our Savior passed three days and three nights in the heart of the earth, so you in your first ascent out of the water represented the first day of Christ in the earth, and by your descent, the night. At night no one can see, but by day one remains in the light. So your descent was like the night: You saw nothing. But in ascending you were as in the day. At the same moment you were both dying and being born. That water of salvation was at once your grave and your mother. And what Solomon said of others will suit you, too. He said that there is "a time to be born, and a time to die" (Eccl 3:2). In your case, however, the order is reversed: There was a time to die and a time to be born; one moment brought both of these about, and your birth came simultaneously with your death.

What a strange and inconceivable thing! We didn't really die. We weren't really buried. We weren't really crucified and raised again. We imitated these symbolically — yet our salvation was a reality! Christ was actually crucified, and actually buried, and truly rose again; and all these things He has freely bestowed upon us, so that we, who share His sufferings by imitation, might gain salvation in reality.

O surpassing loving-kindness! Christ received nails in His undefiled hands and feet, and suffered anguish. Meanwhile, He freely gives me salvation, without pain or toil, by the fellowship of His suffering.

Let no one suppose, then, that baptism is just the grace of remission of sins, with adoption added, as John's was a baptism conferring only the remission of sins. No, we know full well that it purges our sins and gives us the gift of the Holy Spirit — but it is also the sacramental sign of Christ's suffering. For this reason, Paul just now cried aloud and said, "Do you not know that all of us who have been baptized into Christ Jesus were baptized into His death? We were buried therefore with Him by baptism into death" (Rom 6:3-4). These words he spoke to some who were inclined to think that baptism gives us the remission of sins and adoption, but not also a share, by imitation, of Christ's true suffering.

Take It to Prayer

⤳❧❧⤳

We didn't really die. We weren't really buried. We weren't really crucified and raised again. We imitated these sym-bolically — yet our salvation was a reality!

Christ received nails in His undefiled hands and feet, and He freely gives me salvation without pain or toil, by the fellowship of His suffering.

The Christian life entails suffering, which is the living out of our baptism.

Learn It by Heart

⤳❧❧⤳

That water of salvation was at once your grave and your mother.

Apply It to Your Life

⤳❧❧⤳

To share God's life means that we also must share the cross of the God-Man. What is our attitude toward hardships that come our way? We have received the grace to bear hardships; we must ever more correspond to that grace. We must learn to accept the cross as Jesus did.

12

~~e9e~~

St. Cyril of Jerusalem

Planted in a Death Like His

Again, when St. Cyril speaks of Christ's burial "in this place," he means the actual tomb of Christ, the centerpiece of the Church of the Holy Sepulcher in Jerusalem. But, no matter where we have been baptized, we have been "planted" together with the true Vine. His suffering, death, and burial were real. Our burial is a likeness to His; but our rising to salvation is real.

Whatever Christ endured "for us men and for our salvation," He suffered it all in reality and not just in appearance. In order that we might learn this, and learn also that we share Christ's sufferings, Paul cried out the truth with great precision: For if we have been "planted" together with Him in a death like His, we shall certainly be united with Him in a resurrection like His (see Rom 6:5). He put it well when he said "planted together." The true Vine was planted in this place; and we, too, by the baptism of death, have been planted together with Him. Ponder the words of the apostle. He didn't say, "For if we have been planted together with His death," but "with a death like His." In Christ's case, there was death in reality, for His soul was really separated from His body, and a real burial took place, for His holy body was wrapped in pure linen; and everything really happened to Him. In your case, however, there was only a likeness of death and sufferings. Yet, as far as salvation is concerned, there was not a likeness but a reality.

I beg you: Now that you have learned these things, keep them in your memory, so that I, who am unworthy, may say of you that I love you "because you remember me in everything and maintain the traditions even as I have delivered them to you" (1 Cor 11:2). God has presented you as those "who have been brought from death to life" (Rom 6:13), and He is able to grant you to "walk in newness of life" (Rom 6:4). For His is the glory and the power, now and for ever. Amen.

Take It to Prayer

If we have been "planted" together with the true Vine in a death like His, we shall certainly be united with Him in a resurrection like His.

In your case, there was only a likeness of death and sufferings. Yet, as far as salvation is concerned, there was not a likeness but a reality.

Now that you have learned these things, keep them in your memory.

Learn It by Heart

꙳ꙮ꙳

The true Vine was planted in this place; and we, too, by the baptism of death, have been planted together with Him.

Apply It to Your Life

꙳ꙮ꙳

Resolve to review, every day, the doctrines you have learned, to "keep them in your memory," to put down deep roots where you have been planted with Christ.

13

St. Cyril of Jerusalem

You Are Other Christs

Cyril here speaks of the sacrament of confirmation, the "second anointing." In fourth-century Jerusalem, confirmation was usually administered just after baptism. (The timing and sequence of the sacraments have varied throughout history and throughout the world, and the Church permits such diversity even today.) Confirmation was also called "chrismation," after holy chrism, the mixture of olive oil and balm used in anointing. The blessed chrism has the power to confer a share of Christ's divinity. The word "chrism" and the word "Christ" come from the same Greek root — christos — which literally means "anointed." When we receive the sacraments of initiation, we are "christened." This is true in two senses: We are anointed, and we are united with God's Anointed One, Jesus Christ.

Since you've been baptized into Christ, and you've put on Christ, you have been conformed to the Son of God. For God, having predestined us to be adopted as His children, conformed us to the body of Christ's glory. Since you have partaken in Christ, you are rightly called "christs," that is, anointed ones. It was about you that God said, "Touch not my anointed ones," my christs (Ps 105:15). Now you have been made christs, by receiving the sacramental sign of the Holy Spirit. Everything has been worked in you by imitation, because you are images of Christ.

He washed in the river Jordan, and having given of the fragrance of His godhead to the waters, He came up from them. Then the Holy Spirit, in the fullness of His being, landed on Him — like resting upon like. In a similar way, after you had come up from the pool of the sacred streams, you were given an ointment, the sign of the anointing Christ received; and this is the Holy Spirit, of whom the blessed Isaiah prophesied in the voice of the Lord: "The Spirit of the Lord GOD is upon me, because the LORD has anointed me to bring good tidings to the afflicted" (Is 61:1).

For Christ was not anointed by human hands with oil or ointment; but the Father, who appointed Him to be the Savior of the whole world, anointed Him with the Holy Spirit. As Peter says: "God anointed Jesus of Nazareth with the Holy Spirit" (Acts 10:38). The prophet David also cried out: "Your divine throne endures for ever and ever. Your royal scepter is a scepter of equity; you love righteousness and hate wickedness. Therefore God, your God, has anointed you with the oil of gladness above your fellows" (Ps 45:6-7).

Christ was really crucified, buried, raised. In baptism, you are counted worthy of being crucified, buried, and raised together with Him, in a likeness. So it is, again, with the chrism. Christ was anointed with a mystical oil of gladness; that is, the Holy Spirit, called the "oil of gladness" because He is the author of spiritual joy. You were anointed with chrism, because you have become sharers and friends of Christ.

Beware of supposing this chrism to be plain ointment. The bread of the Eucharist, after the invocation of the Holy Spirit, is no longer mere bread; it is the Body of Christ. So, too, this holy chrism, after the invocation, is no longer a common ointment; it is Christ's gift of grace, and by the power of the Holy Spirit it is able to share His divinity.

Take It to Prayer

Christ was not anointed by human hands with oil, but by the Father, who anointed Him with the Holy Spirit.

You were anointed with chrism, because you have become sharers and friends of Christ.

Since you have partaken in Christ, you are rightly called "christs."

Learn It by Heart

Holy chrism, after the invocation, is no longer a common ointment; it is Christ's gift of grace, and by the power of the Holy Spirit it is able to share His divinity.

Apply It to Your Life

If you have become another "christ," your life is now charged with power from God — power to co-redeem with Christ, power to suffer for the sake of others, power to give witness, and to offer your daily labor as a work of God. What you do and say may appear ordinary, but so does the ointment that empowered you to share in Christ's divinity.

14

St. Cyril of Jerusalem

The Right to Be Called "Christian"

In the Church of Jerusalem, the sacrament of confirmation, or "chrismation," included a thorough anointing of the senses, renewing them for Christian life.

This ointment is symbolically applied to your forehead and your other senses. And while your body is anointed with the visible ointment, your soul is made holy by the Holy and life-giving Spirit.

You were first anointed on the forehead, that you might be delivered from the shame that the first man who sinned bore about with him everywhere. With unveiled face you might reflect, like a mirror, the glory of the Lord (see 2 Cor 3:18). Then you are anointed on your ears, that you might receive ears that are quick to hear the divine mysteries. As Isaiah said: The Lord gave me an ear to hear (see Is 50:4-5). And the Lord Jesus in the Gospel said: "He who has ears to hear, let him hear" (Mt 11:15).

Then you were anointed on the nostrils, so that receiving the sacred ointment you may say: "For we are the aroma of Christ to God among those who are being saved" (2 Cor 2:15). Afterwards, you were anointed on your breast, and you "put on the breastplate of righteousness ... that you may be able to stand against the wiles of the devil" (Eph 6:14, 11). Now, Christ went forth, after His baptism and the visitation of the Holy Spirit, and He vanquished the enemy. So you, too, after holy baptism and the mystical chrism — after putting on the whole armor of the Holy Spirit — so you, too, must stand firm against the power of the enemy, and vanquish it, saying, "I can do all things in the Christ, the anointed, who strengthens me" (see Phil 4:13).

Now deemed worthy of this holy chrism, you are called "Christians," a new name to suit your new birth. Before you were worthy of this grace, you had no right to this title, but were advancing on your way toward being Christians.

You should know that this chrism was prefigured in the Old Testament. When Moses gave his brother the command of God and made him high priest, he anointed him after washing him in water. Then Aaron was called "christ" or "anointed," clearly named after the figurative chrism. And again, when the high priest raised Solomon to kingship, he anointed him after he had bathed in Gihon. To them, however, these things happened figuratively, but to you there is nothing figurative. It's the truth, because you were truly anointed by the Holy Spirit. Christ is the beginning of your salvation; for He is truly the first-fruit, while you are the whole lump of dough. But "if the dough offered as first fruits is holy, so is the whole lump" (Rom 11:16).

Keep this anointing unspotted, for it shall teach you all things, but only if it remains in you, as you have heard declared by the blessed John (see 1 Jn 2:27), who had much to say concerning this chrism. For this holy thing is a spiritual safeguard for the body and salvation for the soul.

Keep this anointing unspotted and unblemished in you. Press forward by good works, and become well-pleasing to the captain of your salvation, Christ Jesus, to whom be glory for ever and ever. Amen.

Take It to Prayer

While your body is anointed with the visible ointment, your soul is made holy by the Holy and life-giving Spirit.

Stand firm against the power of the enemy, and vanquish it, saying, "I can do all things in the Christ, the anointed, who strengthens me."

Now deemed worthy of this holy chrism, you are called "Christians," a new name to suit your new birth.

Learn It by Heart

This holy thing is a spiritual safeguard for the body and salvation for the soul.

Apply It to Your Life

With the sacrament of confirmation, we gain the full right to be called "Christian." With rights come duties. We have a duty to guard our senses, which have been anointed by the Holy Spirit, and never willingly or carelessly expose them to sinful things.

WEEK 3

with St. Clement of Alexandria

On Illumination

Titus Flavius Clemens was born sometime around 150, probably near the city of Athens, Greece. We know little of his early life, though we can surmise that he was a seeker after truth, and he read voraciously. St. Clement's writings display his easy familiarity with the classics of Greek literature, as well as the current state of the sciences and the customs of the major world religions.

In adulthood, Clement converted to Christianity. He devoured all the available books of Christian literature. Soon, he was more fluent in the Old and New Testaments than he was in the Greek poets and philosophers. He resolved to learn the faith from the greatest teacher he could find. He traveled through the lands of the eastern Mediterranean and studied with spiritual masters in each place. In Alexandria, Egypt, he "found rest" when he found Pantaenus, the man who had established the great Christian school in that city.

Alexandria was the intellectual capital of the world. There was a superabundance of schools there, and teachers, and well-off, well-educated men and women who had the leisure time to study.

Clement set himself the task of converting these chattering classes. He spoke to them in the language they understood, drawing from the literature and sciences he, too, had studied. He applied the philosophy of ancient Greece to his systematic presentation of Christian doctrine.

He exhorted ordinary Christians to study deeply in the Christian mysteries and cultivate a disciplined life of contemplation and prayer. He emphasized the role of "knowledge" in the progress of the soul, and the role of good morals in purifying the soul to be a worthy vessel of divine knowledge. The instructed Christian, he believed, could more easily be perfected on earth, and so reach a greater degree of union with God.

In his lectures, Clement could soar to the heights of mystical and philosophical speculation. Yet he was always able to come down to earth with practical advice. He spoke with sensitivity and keen insight about family life, the deep friendship of husband and wife, and even sexual morality. Though he often drew from the best of pagan learning, his lectures always — always — found their grounding in the Scriptures.

Around 200, Clement succeeded his teacher, Pantaenus, as head of the Alexandrian school. But within a short space of time, he was driven away by persecution. He found refuge at Caesarea in Cappadocia (in modern Turkey) with an Alexandrian alumnus named Alexander. It is from a letter of Alexander's that we know St. Clement was dead by the year 215. He was never able to return to Egypt.

From the time of his death, he was venerated as a teacher and a saint.

15

St. Clement of Alexandria

Be Perfect

Baptism was known by many names in the ancient Church. St. Clement considers them, one by one. He speaks of the "perfection" that comes to us with divine life. Perfection is a dynamic process that allows stages of growth. Christ was a perfect infant, toddler, boy, teen, and adult. God's life is absolute perfection; each stage of God's life growing in us is relative perfection.

We are called "children" and "infants," but not because our education is childish and contemptible. On the contrary, when we were reborn we immediately attained that perfection we had been striving for. For we were illuminated, which is to know God. And surely anyone who knows the Perfect One is not imperfect.

Baptized, we are illuminated; illuminated, we become sons; becoming sons, we are made perfect; made perfect, we become immortal. He says: "You are gods, sons of the Most High, all of you" (Ps 82:6). This action is called by many names: grace [or gift], illumination, perfection, and washing. It is the washing by which we cleanse away our sins. It is the grace by which the penalties for our sins are waived. And it is the illumination by which we see salvation's holy light — by which we see God clearly.

Now we call something perfect when it lacks nothing. And what is lacking to someone who knows God? For it would be truly odd to call something incomplete a gift from God. Because He is perfect, He bestows perfect gifts. At His command all things were made; so when He merely wishes to bestow grace, there arises the perfection of His grace. What is still to come is here foreshadowed by the power of His will.

And release from evil is only the beginning of salvation. We alone — we who first have touched the very end of life — are already perfect. And we already live who are separated from death. Salvation, then, is the following of Christ: "In him was life" (Jn 1:4). "Truly, truly, I say to you, he who hears my word and believes him who sent me, has eternal life; he does not come into judgment, but has passed from death to life" (Jn 5:24). So just the fact of believing and being reborn is perfection in life. For God is never weak. As His will is His work, and this is called the universe; so, too, His wish is the salvation of everyone, and this has been called the Church. He knows whom He has called, and whom He has saved; and He called and saved them at the same time (see Rom 8:30).

The apostle says: "For you yourselves have been taught by God" (1 Thess 4:9). It is not permitted, then, to consider His teaching imperfect. That teaching is the eternal salvation of the eternal Savior, to whom be thanks for ever and ever. Amen. And he who is merely reborn and is enlightened — as the name itself indicates —is delivered from darkness, and immediately receives the light.

It is like those who have shaken off sleep and become all awake inside; or like those who, temporarily blinded, have an obstruction removed from their eyes. In the same way, once we have wiped away the sins that obscure the light of the Divine Spirit, we who are baptized gain a spiritual sight that is free, unimpeded, and full of light — the sort of light that alone enables us to contemplate the divine: the Holy Spirit flowing down to us from above.

This is the eternal correction of the vision, now able to see the eternal light. For like attracts like; and holiness attracts the very source of holiness, who is rightly called the Light (see Jn 1:4-5). "For once you were darkness, but now you are light in the Lord" (Eph 5:8).

Still, they object, man has not yet received the gift of perfection. I agree; but I would add that he is already in the light, and the darkness has not overcome him (see Jn 1:5). There is nothing halfway between light and darkness. But the end is reserved till the resurrection of believers. And the end is not the reception of something else, but the fulfillment of the promise already made.

These two cannot happen simultaneously: the arrival at the end, and the expectation of that arrival. For eternity and time are not the same. Nor is the attempt the same as the final result. But both refer to the same thing, and the same person is involved in both. Faith is the attempt, begun in time; the final result is the reaching of the promise, secured for eternity.

We await in advance what we have already grasped by faith, and after the resurrection we will receive it in full. All this is to fulfill what was said: "According to your faith be it done to you" (Mt 9:29).

Take It to Prayer

❧

This is the one grace of illumination: that our characters are not the same as before our washing.

We await in advance what we have already grasped by faith, and after the resurrection we will receive it in full.

His wish is the salvation of everyone, and this has been called the Church.

Learn It by Heart

❧

Like attracts like; and holiness attracts the very source of holiness, who is rightly called the Light.

Apply It to Your Life

❧

Is our faith as robust as it should be — as it must be, if we are to live by it? Pray daily the prayer of the apostles: "Increase our faith!" (Lk 17:5).

16

St. Clement of Alexandria

The Milk of Mother Church

St. Clement compares the Eucharist to a mother's nourishment of her infant child. As a mother feeds her baby from her own substance, so does Mother Church feed God's children with the body, blood, soul, and divinity of Jesus Christ.

We have still to explain what the apostle said: "I fed you with milk, not solid food; for you were not ready for it; and even yet you are not ready" (1 Cor 3:2).

As nursing mothers nourish newborn children on milk, so do I also by the Word, the milk of Christ, give you spiritual nourishment. I have given you the knowledge that nourishes to life eternal.

Now that the kind and loving Father has rained down the Word, it is He Himself who has become the spiritual nourishment to the saints. O mystic marvel! The Father of all is one, and one is the Word who belongs to all; and the Holy Spirit is one and the same everywhere. And one is the only virgin mother — I love to call her the Church. This mother, when alone, had no milk, because alone she was not a wife. But she is at once virgin and mother — pure as a virgin, loving as a mother. Calling her children to her, she nurses them with holy milk, with the Word for childhood. That is why she had no milk; for the milk was this child, fair and beautiful, the body of Christ. She nourishes this young brood upon the Word, which the Lord Himself brought forth in throes of the flesh, which the Lord Himself clothed in His precious blood.

O amazing birth! O holy swaddling clothes! The Word is everything to the child, father and mother and tutor and nurse. "Eat my flesh," He says, "and drink my blood" (see Jn 6:53-57). He Himself is the food He gives. He offers His flesh and pours forth His blood, and nothing more is needed for the children's growth.

O amazing mystery. We are invited to cast off the old bodily corruption, and with it our former nourishment, and receive in exchange another new way of life — Christ's! We must hide Him within, enshrining the Savior in our souls, so that we may be rid of the passions of our flesh.

Take It to Prayer

The Father is one, the Word is one, and the Holy Spirit is one. And one is the only virgin mother — I love to call her the Church.

The Word is everything to the child, father and mother and tutor and nurse. He Himself is the food He gives.

We must hide Him within, enshrining the Savior in our souls.

Learn It by Heart

❦

The Word Himself has become the spiritual nourishment to the saints.

Apply It to Your Life

❦

Make the most of the moments after you receive Holy Communion. Don't rush out of church. Thank God for the great gift of Himself. Praise Him. Speak to Him of your most pressing needs.

17

St. Clement of Alexandria

One Lord, One Church

St. Clement reveals the Catholic Church as the one true Church.

The true Church, the really ancient Church, is one. In it are enrolled those who are just by God's design. God is one, and the Lord is one, so what is most honorable is praised because of its singleness, its imitation of the one first principle. In the nature of the One, then, is the heritage of the one Church. Therefore, in substance and idea, in origin, in eminence, we say that the ancient and Catholic Church is alone, gathering into the unity of the one faith — the faith that comes from the two Covenants, or rather the one Covenant in different times by the will of the one God, and through the one Lord — those already chosen, whom God predestined, knowing before the foundation of the world that they would be righteous. The eminence of the Church, in its unity and as the principle of union, surpasses all things and has no equal.

Take It to Prayer

The true Church, the really ancient Church, is one.

The ancient and Catholic Church stands alone, gathering the many into the unity of the one faith.

The Church stands as the principle of union.

Learn It by Heart

In the nature of the One God is the heritage of the one Church.

Apply It to Your Life

Love the Church by showing respect for the symbols of its unity, the people who hold the Church together: the Catholic hierarchy, the pope, the bishops. Avoid cynical or disrespectful speech about the Church, and gently correct others who speak that way.

18

St. Clement of Alexandria

The Sacred Vine, the Eucharist

Though Clement wrote this passage between the years 200 and 215, Catholics today will recognize it as a poetic meditation on the Mass. In a very brief space, Clement weaves images from the ritual with allusions to the most famous eucharistic passages of the New Testament (see Jn 6, 1 Cor 10-11, and the accounts of the Last Supper in Matthew, Mark, and Luke).

The sacred vine produced the prophetic cluster. The great cluster, the Word, was bruised for us. For the blood of the grape — that is, the Word — wanted to be mixed with water, as His blood is mingled with salvation.

And the blood of the Lord is twofold. For there is the blood of His flesh, by which we are redeemed from corruption; and there is the blood that is spiritual, by which we are anointed. To drink the blood of Jesus is to partake of the Lord's immortality. The Spirit is the power of the Word, as blood is the power of the body.

So, as wine is blended with water, so is the Spirit with man. And the one, the mixture of wine and water, nourishes us to faith; while the other, the Spirit, conducts us to immortality.

And the mixture of both — of the water and of the Word — is called the Eucharist, the renowned and glorious gift. And those who faithfully receive it are made holy both in body and soul. For it is the Father's will that man — himself composed by God of body and soul — should be mystically united to the Spirit and the Word. For truly the Spirit is joined to the soul, who depends upon Him; and the flesh is joined to the flesh, for whom the Word became flesh (see Jn 1:14).

Take It to Prayer

Those who faithfully receive the Eucharist are made holy both in body and soul.

To drink the blood of Jesus is to partake of the Lord's immortality.

The flesh is joined to the flesh, for whom the Word became flesh.

Learn It by Heart

"The cup of blessing which we bless, is it not a participation in the blood of Christ?" (1 Cor 10:16).

Apply It to Your Life

The Eucharist is our source of joy. Next time we're weighed down by sadness or anxiety, we should remember the nearness of God, who keeps us closer than a mother keeps her child.

19

St. Clement of Alexandria

The Good Father God

Clement harbors no romantic illusions about human family life, to which the world births us badly. He reminds us, however, that we have been born again into a new family — God's family — with a good Father who will never fail us.

Hear the Savior: "I gave you a new birth, you whom the world birthed badly for death. I freed you, healed you, ransomed you. I will show you the face of the good Father God. Call no man your father on earth. Let the dead bury the dead. But follow Me. For I will bring you to a rest of ineffable and unutterable blessings, which eye has not seen, nor ear heard, nor have they entered into the heart of men — things that angels desire to look into, and see what good things God has prepared for the saints and the children who love Him. I am He who feeds you, giving Myself as bread. And he who has tasted this bread experiences death no more. And every day I supply the drink of immortality. I am teacher of heavenly lessons. For you I fought with death, and paid the price of your death, which you owed for your former sins and your unbelief toward God."

Take It to Prayer

~~≈≈~~

"I gave you a new birth, you whom the world birthed badly for death."

"I will show you the face of the good Father God."

"For you I fought with death, and paid the price of your death, which you owed for your former sins."

Learn It by Heart

~~≈≈~~

"Every day I supply the drink of immortality. I am teacher of heavenly lessons."

Apply It to Your Life

~~≈≈~~

No matter how deeply or how often we have been disappointed by earthly men we've called "father," we must not project their failings onto God. Our Father God is the measure by which we know the shortcomings of earthly dads and earthly clergy; for their vocation is to be His image on earth. God allows them to fail so that we might seek perfect fatherhood in Him.

20

St. Clement of Alexandria

How to Live Like a Christian

Clement gave the following address to newly baptized Christians whom he had instructed. It sketches out, in fine and sensitive detail, a way of Christian life in the world.

Cultivate quietness in word and deed, in the way you speak and carry yourself.

Avoid rash eagerness. For then the mind will remain steady, and won't be agitated by your eagerness, won't grow weak and narrow and dim. Nor will it be weakened by gluttony, by boiling rage, or by the other passions, lying a ready prey to them. For the mind, seated on high on a quiet throne, looking intently toward God, must control the passions.

By no means be swept away by temper in bursts of anger, nor be sluggish in speaking, nor nervous in movement; so that your quietness may be adorned by good proportion and your bearing may appear something divine and sacred. Guard also against the signs of arrogance: a haughty bearing, a lofty head, a dainty and high-treading footstep.

Let your speech be gentle toward those you meet, and your greetings kind. Be modest toward the opposite sex, and let your glance be turned to the ground. Be thoughtful in all your talk, and give back a useful answer, adapting the words to the hearer's need, just so loud that it may be distinctly audible, neither escaping the ears of the company by reason of feebleness, nor going to excess with too much noise.

Take care never to speak what you have not weighed and pondered beforehand; nor interject your own words on the spur of the moment and in the midst of another's; for you must listen and converse in turn, with set times for speech and for silence. Learn gladly, and teach ungrudgingly; never hide wisdom from others by reason of a grudging spirit, nor through false modesty stand aloof from instruction. Submit to elders just as to parents. Honor God's servants. Be first to practice wisdom and virtue. Do not wrangle with your friends, nor mock at them and play the buffoon. Firmly renounce falsehood, guile, and insolence. Endure the arrogant and insolent in silence, like a gentle and high-minded person.

Let everything you do be done for God, both deeds and words; and refer all that is yours to Christ; and constantly turn your soul to God; and lean your thought on the power of Christ, as if in some harbor by the divine light of the Savior it were resting from all talk and action.

And often by day speak your thoughts to men, but most of all to God at night as well as by day. Don't let too much sleep keep you from your prayers and hymns to God, since long sleep is a rival of death. Show yourself always a partner of Christ, who makes the divine ray shine from heaven. Let Christ be to you continual and unceasing joy.

Do not relax the tension of your soul with feasting and drunkenness, but consider what is needful to be enough for the body. And do not rush early to meals, before the time for dinner comes; but let your dinner be bread, and let earth's grasses and the ripe fruits of trees be set before you; and go to your meal with composure, showing no sign of raging gluttony. In place of such pleasures, choose the joys that are in divine words and hymns, joys supplied to you by wisdom from God; and let heavenly meditation ever lead you upward to heaven.

And give up the many anxious cares about the body by taking comfort in hopes toward God; because for you He will provide enough of all the necessary things: food to support life, covering for the body, and protection against winter cold. For to your King belongs the whole earth and all that is produced from it; and God treats the bodily parts of His servants with exceeding care, as if they were His, like His own shrines and temples. On this account do not dread severe diseases, nor the approach of old age, which must be expected in time; for even disease will come to an end, when with wholehearted purpose we do His commandments.

Knowing this, make your soul strong even in the face of diseases. Be courageous, like a man in the arena, bravest to submit to his toils with strength unmoved. Don't be utterly crushed in soul by grief, whether disease lies heavily upon you or any other hardship befalls you, but nobly confront labors with your understanding. And give thanks to God, even in the midst of your struggles, because His thoughts are wiser than ours, so much so that they are not easy or possible to discern.

Pity those who are in distress, and ask for all the help that comes from God; for God will grant grace to His friend who asks, and will relieve those in distress. He wishes to make His power known to men, in hope that, when they have come to full knowledge, they may return to God, and may enjoy eternal blessedness when the Son of God shall appear and restore good things to His own.

Take It to Prayer

Show yourself always a partner of Christ, who makes the divine ray shine from heaven. Let Christ be your continual and unceasing joy.

Do not be swept away by temper, nor be sluggish in speaking, nor nervous in movement. May your bearing appear something divine and sacred.

Give thanks to God, even in the midst of your struggles, because His thoughts are wiser than ours, so much so that they are not easy or possible to discern.

Learn It by Heart

Let everything you do be done for God, both deeds and words.

Apply It to Your Life

Take care never to speak what you have not weighed and pondered beforehand. Make a habit of stopping to think.

21

St. Clement of Alexandria

The Power of Prayer

Prayer doesn't change God. He is unchanging and unchangeable. But it does change us, making us more like Him, and thus more able to accept His will, whatever it may be. Prayer makes us radiate goodness.

On the face of Moses there settled a kind of glorified hue, because of his righteous conduct and his constant conversation with God who spoke to him. So, too, a divine power of goodness clings to the righteous soul in contemplation, in prophecy, and in the act of governing. It impresses on the soul a kind of intellectual radiance, like a ray of the sun, as a visible sign of righteousness. It unites the soul with light, through unbroken love, which is God-bearing and borne by God. This is how someone who knows God grows in likeness to God the Savior, as far as human nature may, since he becomes perfect "as your heavenly Father is perfect" (Mt 5:48).

Take It to Prayer

A divine power of goodness clings to the righteous soul in contemplation.

"If ... the Israelites could not look at Moses' face because of its brightness, fading as this was, will not the dispensation of the Spirit be attended with greater splendor?" (2 Cor 3:7–8).

"All of us, gazing with unveiled face on the glory of the Lord, are being transformed into the same image from glory to glory" (2 Cor 3:18, NAB).

Learn It by Heart

Prayer is how someone who knows God grows in likeness to God.

Apply It to Your Life

Schedule time for prayer each day. Make it the most important appointment on your calendar. Stick to it.

WEEK 4

with St. Ambrose of Milan

On the Eucharist

Great scholars and saints count St. Ambrose (340-397) among the most excellent preachers of mystagogy in all the history of the Church. His teaching seems even more remarkable when one considers the very unusual circumstances of Ambrose's own Christian initiation.

He was born into a noble Roman family that had long before converted to Christianity. Ambrose's father was prefect over one of the largest and most important territories in the empire, ranging through Britain, France, Spain, and Africa.

Ambrose was trained as a lawyer and was soon retracing the career of his illustrious father. While still a young man, Ambrose was appointed by the emperor to be a consular governor, residing in Milan, Italy, which was then the most important city in the west.

Though Ambrose came from a devout family, his parents — like many at that time — deferred his baptism. It was as governor in Milan that he began his serious study of the faith, intending to be baptized.

One thing is certain: He could not study in peace. The Church in Milan — and so all the people in Milan — were divided over doctrinal matters. One bishop had been exiled in chains. His successor, an Arian heretic, arrived from the East and could not speak the local language. This interloper ruthlessly persecuted the Milanese who professed faith in

Christ's divinity. When the man died, the Catholics rejoiced, but they worried over who would replace him. Moreover, the Arians in Milan were determined to elevate another one of their own.

As governor, Ambrose feared that the argument would soon get bloody, so he intervened to try to negotiate peace. His efforts worked all too well. Both the Arians and the Catholics came to peaceful terms. They agreed, unanimously, that Ambrose should be their bishop — Ambrose, who was not yet baptized.

Ambrose disagreed with them, but the emperor sided with the people of Milan, and so, a week later, Ambrose received all the sacraments of initiation — baptism, Eucharist, and confirmation — along with the fullness of holy orders.

Ambrose set himself to restoring discipline to the clergy, unity to the Church, and dignity to his office. Like Basil, he refused, on principle, to respond to the imperial summons. He refused also to give the Arian empress a basilica for heretical worship. And he even dared to impose severe public penance on an emperor for ordering a brutal massacre of civilians.

Ambrose was known the world over for his intelligence. This is the quality that first attracted a young African professor named Augustine to seek the bishop's company. But Augustine came to admire Ambrose's generosity most of all. Ambrose, a busy man, befriended the young Augustine and gently convinced him of the truth of Christianity. Ambrose was the mystagogical teacher to Augustine, who became possibly the greatest theologian in Christian history.

Ambrose's mystagogy is profoundly scriptural, deeply liturgical. It continues to speak to modern Western readers, as many of the Mass's prayers have remained the same through these sixteen hundred years.

St. Ambrose died on Good Friday in 397.

~ ❧ ~

22

St. Ambrose of Milan

A Nation of Priests

St. Ambrose showed the newly baptized the deepest roots of the Christian rites. In the Old Covenant, only God's elite corps, His priests, could enter the Temple's sanctuary. Only the high priest could enter the Holy of Holies, and even he could enter on only one day each year. Now Christ the high priest has entered the Holy of Holies to stay, and He has made His Church a nation of priests, admitted with Him to the Holy of Holies from the moment of their rebirth.

In the Old Testament, the priests would enter continually into the first tabernacle. Into the second tabernacle, the high priest entered once a year. In that second tabernacle was the manna; there was also the rod of Aaron that withered and then blossomed again; and there was the incense (see Heb 9:4-7).

What is the meaning of this? So that you might understand the second tabernacle, into which the high priest introduced you, the tabernacle that the high priest enters once a year — that is, the baptistery, where the rod of Aaron blossomed; it was withered before, but afterward it blossomed again. You, too, were withered, and now you begin to blossom again in the streaming font. You had withered through sins, through faults and trespasses; but now you begin to bear fruit, "planted by streams of water" (Ps 1:3).

Perhaps you say, "What has this to do with the people, if the priest's rod had withered and blossomed again?" Yet what is the people itself but priestly? It was to this people that the apostle Peter said: "You are a chosen race, a royal priesthood, a holy nation" (1 Pet 2:9). Everyone is anointed to the priesthood and also anointed to the kingdom; but it is a spiritual kingdom and a spiritual priesthood.

In the second tabernacle there was a bowl of incense, too, which sent forth a sweet fragrance. So you also are now the sweet "aroma of Christ" (2 Cor 2:15). No longer do you have any share of sins or any odor of error.

Take It to Prayer

You had withered through sins, but now you begin to blossom again in the streaming font.

"You are a chosen race, a royal priesthood, a holy nation" (1 Pet 2:9).

You are the sweet "aroma of Christ" (2 Cor 2:15).

Learn It by Heart

Everyone is anointed to the priesthood and also anointed to the kingdom; but it is a spiritual kingdom and a spiritual priesthood.

Apply It to Your Life

You are a royal priest because you share in the kingship and priesthood of Jesus Christ. A priest's job is to mediate between God and man and offer sacrifice. Your sacrifice is your entire day, your entire life. Make a habit of offering your day to God, from the moment you rise out of bed. Learn one of the Church's traditional "Morning Offering" prayers.

23

St. Ambrose of Milan

Keeping Company with Angels

Why are we baptized? Because we want to be united with Christ forever in heaven. We don't, however, have to wait for our death. That union of body and soul begins now in the sacrament of Holy Communion. There, even the angels marvel at what we are given. We could not receive the gift, though, if we had not first been purified.

Then you came to the altar. You began to approach; the angels watched. They saw you; and your human nature, which before had been stained with the murky filth of sin, suddenly shone bright in their sight. And so they said, "Who is that coming from the wilderness washed so white?" (see Sgs 8:5). The angels marvel! Do you know what they find so marvelous? The apostle Peter said that you have received things that even angels long to see (see 1 Pet 1:12); and Paul said, "What no eye has seen, nor ear heard, nor the heart of man conceived, what God has prepared for those who love Him" (1 Cor 2:9).

Think about what you have received. Holy David, the prophet, saw this grace foretold, and he wanted it. Do you know how much he wanted it? Listen to him saying, "Purge me with hyssop, and I shall be clean; wash me, and I shall be whiter than snow" (Ps 51:7). Why? Because snow is white, but it quickly turns black and filthy with any dirt. But if you hold fast to the grace you have received, it will be lasting and eternal.

So you came with desire to the altar, because you had seen so much grace. You came with desire to the altar to receive the sacrament. Let your soul say, "I will go in to the altar of God: to God who giveth joy to my youth" (Ps 43:4, DR). You have taken off the old age of sins. You have taken on the youth of grace. All this the heavenly sacraments gave to you. So listen again to David: "Your youth is renewed like the eagle's" (Ps 103:5). You have begun to be a good eagle, seeking heaven, scorning earthly things. Good eagles stay close to the altar; for "Wherever the body is, there the eagles will be gathered together" (Mt 24:28). The altar itself is a symbol of the body, and the body of Christ is on the altar. You are eagles, renewed by the washing away of sin.

Take It to Prayer

You came to the altar, and your human nature, which had been stained with sin, suddenly shone bright in the sight of the angels.

You have taken on the youth of grace. All this the heavenly sacraments gave to you.

If you hold fast to the grace you have received, it will be lasting and eternal.

Learn It by Heart

~~≈≈~~

You have received things that even angels long to see.

Apply It to Your Life

~~≈≈~~

Pray to your guardian angel every day. Strive to grow more aware of all the angels. They are always present with you, but especially when you attend the Mass. There, you are surrounded by countless angels of heaven.

24

St. Ambrose of Milan

Words of Power

St. Ambrose develops an idea we encountered earlier, in the preaching of St. Gregory of Nyssa; that is, the sacramental principle. The most ordinary things in the world, at God's bidding, can serve as vessels of extraordinary power, divine power. This happens, by the will of God and the work of the Holy Spirit, through the words of consecration. The Word of God, spoken in the Spirit by His anointed minister, has the power to create, to transfigure, to "do" what it says it is doing. Because these words are God's, they have the power to transform matter and even to call forth something out of nothing. St. Ambrose traces the precedents for this mystery to the very beginning of time.

Perhaps you say, "The bread I see is ordinary bread." Yes, it is bread before the words of the sacraments. But when consecration has been added, from bread it becomes the flesh of Christ.

How can bread be the body of Christ? By consecration. But in what words and in whose phrases is the consecration? Those of the Lord Jesus. For all the other things that are said in the earlier parts of the service are said by the priest — praises are offered to God, prayer is asked for the people, for kings, and the rest. But when it comes to the consecration of the venerable sacrament, the priest no longer uses his own language; he uses the phrases of Christ. Therefore, the Word of Christ consecrates this sacrament.

What is the Word of Christ? It is the Word by which all things are made. The Lord commanded, and heaven was made. The Lord commanded, and the earth was made. The Lord commanded, and the seas were made. The Lord commanded, and every creature was produced. You see, then, how effective is the Word of Christ. The Word of the Lord Jesus is so powerful that it can create something out of nothing. It is so powerful that things previously existing should be changed into something else. Heaven did not exist, the sea did not exist, the earth did not exist; but, as David said, "He commanded and they were created" (Ps 148:5).

So I reply to you, it was not the body of Christ before consecration; but after consecration, I tell you, it is now the body of Christ. He spoke, and it was made; He commanded, and it was created. You yourself formerly existed, but you were an old creature; after you were consecrated, you were a new creature. Do you know how you became a new creature? Everyone, it is written, is in Christ a new creation (see 2 Cor 5:17).

The Word of Christ changes every creature and changes the laws of nature whenever He wishes. Take, for example, His own conception. Usually a child is conceived from a man and a woman during ordinary marital relations; but because the Lord wished, because He chose this mystery, Christ was born of the Holy Spirit and the Virgin. So, you see, "mediator between God and men, the man Christ Jesus" (1 Tim 2:5), was born contrary to the laws and course of nature. He was born as a human, but from a virgin.

Listen to another example. The Jews were hard-pressed by the Egyptians (see Ex 14); they were shut in by the sea. At the divine command, Moses touched the waters with his rod, and the waves divided — certainly not by the course of nature, but by the grace of the heavenly command. Listen to another. The people were thirsty (see Ex 15:23-25). They came to the spring. The spring was bitter. Holy Moses cast wood into the spring, and the spring that had been bitter was made sweet — that is, it changed its nature when it received the sweetness of grace. Hear a fourth example. The ax head had fallen into the waters; because it was iron, it sank (see 2 Kings 6:5-6). Elisha threw in a piece of wood, and immediately the iron rose and floated upon the water, contrary to the nature of iron, for iron is heavier than water.

We see, then, that grace has more power than nature, and yet so far we have only spoken of the grace of a prophet's blessing. But if a man's blessing had such power to change nature, what about the divine consecration, where the very words of the Lord and Savior are at work? For that sacrament you receive is made what it is by the Word of Christ. If the word of Elijah had power enough to bring down fire from heaven (1 Kings 18:36-38), shall not the Word of Christ have power to change the nature of the elements?

The Lord Jesus Himself proclaims: "This is My body" (Mt 26:26, Mk 14:22). One nature exists before the blessing of the heavenly words, but after the consecration, the body is signified. He Himself speaks of His blood. Before the consecration it has another name, but after it is called blood.

And you say, "Amen," that is, "It is true!" Let the heart feel what the words say!

— ON THE SACRAMENTS 4.4, ON THE MYSTERIES 9

Take It to Prayer

It is bread before the words of consecration, but afterward it becomes the flesh of Christ.

When it comes to the consecration, the priest no longer uses his own language, but the phrases of Christ. The Word of Christ consecrates this sacrament.

The Word of the Lord Jesus is so powerful that it can create something out of nothing. It is so powerful that things previously existing should be changed into something else.

Learn It by Heart

He spoke, and it was made; He commanded, and it was created.

Apply It to Your Life

Consider the power of God's words, then consider the power of your own. For you have come to share God's life and flesh and blood, to partake in the divine nature. Your words, too, can work with greater power now, for good or for evil. You live in communion with Jesus Christ. He prays in you, and you pray in Him. The words you speak, to God and to others, call down blessings or judgment, upon your-self and upon others. Weigh them carefully.

25

St. Ambrose of Milan

The Testimony of Christ

It is always reassuring to read the words of the Church Fathers describing the Mass, because the Church's doctrine has remained essentially unchanged through two millennia. When we read St. Ambrose, it is striking to note that so many small details of the Church's ritual have also come down to us in familiar forms. The Mass that Ambrose used when he wrote these homilies, in the years 380-390, included many of the same gestures and prayers that we hear today in our parishes. Why is that so? Because they are the same words Jesus uttered over bread and wine at the Last Supper, carefully preserved in the New Testament and in the Church.

Do you want to know how the sacrament is consecrated by heavenly words? Listen to what the priest says: "Bless and approve our offering; make it acceptable to You, an offering in spirit and in truth. Let it become for us the body and blood of Jesus Christ, Your only Son, our Lord. The day before He suffered, He took bread in His sacred hands, and looking up to heaven, to You, His almighty Father, He gave You thanks and praise. He broke the bread, gave it to His disciples, and said: 'Take this, all of you, and eat it: This is My body, which will be given up for you.'

"When supper was ended, He took the cup. Again He gave You thanks and praise, gave the cup to His disciples, and said: 'Take this, all of you, and drink from it: This is the cup of my blood.'"

Notice that all those words, up to "Take" (whether the body or the blood), are from the evangelists. After that, they are the words of Christ: "Take this, all of you, and drink from it: This is the cup of my blood." (See Mt 26:26ff; Mk 14:22ff; Lk 22:19ff; 1 Cor 11:23ff. See also Mk 6:41 and 8:6.)

Look closely into these matters. It says: "The day before He suffered, He took bread in His sacred hands." Before the consecration, it is bread; but when the words of Christ have been added, it is the body of Christ. Then listen to Him say: "Take this, all of you, and eat it: This is My body."

Also, before the words of Christ, the chalice is full of wine and water. But when the words of Christ have been added, it is made the blood of Christ, which redeemed the people. You have seen, in many ways, how the Word of Christ has power to change all things. The Lord Jesus Himself testifies that we receive His body and blood. Should we doubt His trustworthiness and testimony?

Take It to Prayer

~~❧~~

The Lord Jesus Himself testifies that we receive His body and blood. Should we doubt His trustworthiness and testimony?

The Word of Christ has power to change all things.

Look closely into these matters.

Learn It by Heart

~~≪e≫~~

Then listen to Jesus say: "Take this, all of you, and eat it: This is My body."

Apply It to Your Life

~~≪e≫~~

Meditate on the miracle of the Eucharist. It is inexhaustible. Do not allow yourself to think that you have it all figured out. Do not allow it to become yesterday's news. You say, "Amen"; which means, "It is true!" Let the heart feel what the words say! St. Ambrose gives us sage advice: Study and pray over the sacramental mysteries. We must dare to "look closely into these matters."

St. Ambrose of Milan

In Living Memory

The word we translate as "memorial" or "remembrance" meant more in the ancient world than these words suggest to us today. We read, in the Old Testament, that God "remembered His covenant." It's not that He had forgotten it before; it's not as if God can ever forget. But there were times in history when God, for the benefit of His people, renewed and reenacted His covenant with them. It helps us even to get at the root of the English words we use. In the Mass, we "re-call" and "re-member." We call upon the Lord and see Him before us again in His body, His members. The Mass is not a nostalgic looking backward. In the Mass, we quite literally proclaim the death of the Lord until He comes again into our midst.

Know, then, that this is a sacrament, and it was prefigured long before. And learn how great the sacrament is. See what He says: "Every time you do this, you will make a memorial of Me until I come again" (see 1 Cor 11:25-26).

And the priest says: "We … recall His passion, His resurrection from the dead, and His ascension into glory; … and we offer to You … this holy and perfect sacrifice: the bread of life and the cup of eternal salvation. Look with favor on these offerings and accept them as once You accepted the gifts of Your servant Abel, the sacrifice of Abraham, our father in faith, and the bread and wine offered by Your priest Melchisedech."

So every time you receive, what does the apostle say to you? Every time we receive, we proclaim the death of the Lord (see 1 Cor 11:26); if we proclaim His death, we proclaim the remission of sins. If, every time blood is poured forth, it is poured for the remission of sins, I should always receive it, so that my sins may always be forgiven. I, who am always sinning, should always have a remedy.

May the Lord our God preserve for you the grace that He has given you and may He illuminate more fully the eyes that He has opened for you, through His only begotten Son, our Lord God, King and Savior, through whom and with whom He has praise, honor, glory, majesty, power with the Holy Spirit now and forever. Amen.

Take It to Prayer

Every time we receive Communion, we proclaim the death of the Lord.

If the blood is poured forth for the remission of sins, I should always receive it, so that my sins may always be forgiven.

May the Lord our God illuminate more fully the eyes that He has opened for you.

Learn It by Heart

I, who am always sinning, should always have a remedy.

Apply It to Your Life

We should often call to mind the death of the Lord. He died not only for "us" — meaning us billions of people who will live on earth in history — but He died for you in particular, as if you were the only soul who mattered. Your sins in particular were the reason for His death; and His death is the remedy for your sins. So meditate upon His suffering and death, especially on Fridays, because He died on a Friday. Proclaim His death and give thanks for it. A traditional way to do this, in addition to the Mass, is by praying the Stations of the Cross.

27

St. Ambrose of Milan

The Embrace of Love

St. Ambrose evokes the most intimate and ecstatic human experi-
ence, that of married love, and he shows that it is a mere shadow
of the love that is consummated between Christians and Christ in
Holy Communion.

You have come to the altar. The Lord Jesus calls you —
both your soul and the Church — and says, "O that you
would kiss me with the kisses of your mouth!" (Sgs 1:2).

Do you want to prepare for Christ? Nothing is sweeter.

Do you want to do this for your soul? Nothing is more
pleasant.

"O that you would kiss me." He sees that you are
cleansed from all sin, your sins are purged away, and you are
worthy of the heavenly sacrament; and so He invites you to
the heavenly banquet. "O that you would kiss me with the
kisses of your mouth!"

Now your soul sees itself cleansed from sin and worthy
to approach the altar of Christ, and so the body of Christ.
Now your soul has seen the wonderful sacraments and says,
"O that you would kiss me with the kisses of your mouth!"
That is: Let Christ press a kiss upon me.

Why? Because "Your love is better than wine" (Sgs 1:2). That is, the sensations that You provide are better — Your sacraments are better than wine. Though wine brings sweetness, joy, and pleasure, it is but worldly joy, while in You is spiritual pleasure.

Even so long ago, Solomon represented the marriage of Christ and the Church or of the spirit and flesh and soul.

You have come to the altar. You have received the grace of Christ. You have received the heavenly sacraments. The Church rejoices in the redemption of many and is glad with spiritual joy that the members of her household are here dressed in white. You have this in the Song of Songs. In joy she calls Christ, having prepared a banquet that seems worthy of heavenly feasting. So she says: "Let my beloved come into his garden, and eat the fruit of his apple trees" (Sgs 5:1, DR). What are his fruit trees? You became a dry tree in Adam; but now through the grace of Christ you have blossomed into a fruitful tree.

The Lord Jesus willingly accepts and with heavenly care responds to His Church. "I come to my garden. ... I gather my myrrh with my spice, I eat my honeycomb with my honey, I drink my wine with my milk. Eat, O friends, and drink: drink deeply," He says (see Sgs 5:1).

Take It to Prayer

꩜

The world's greatest love poem tells the story of Christ and the Church, of God and humanity.

Washed in baptism, we grow more attractive to our beloved.

Your sacraments are better than wine. Though wine brings sweetness, joy, and pleasure, it is but worldly joy, while in You is spiritual pleasure.

Learn It by Heart

꩜

The Church has prepared a banquet worthy of heavenly feasting, and so she calls upon her beloved, Jesus Christ.

Apply It to Your Life

꩜

Those who are in love are willing to work hard to please their beloved. They choose carefully from their wardrobe. They spend more time at washing and grooming. We can learn much from lovers about how to please God. We should, of course, always strive to keep as spiritually clean as on the day of our baptism. We should show ourselves spiritually ready for the heavenly banquet — for heaven on earth — which is the Mass. We are not disembodied souls, however; and so, when we prepare for Mass, we should also give special care to our physical appearance, grooming and dressing ourselves as well as we can. We should not let our love grow tired or careless. Our bodies are expressions of our souls. Our comportment at Mass is a visible expression of our love for Christ.

28

St. Ambrose of Milan

Our Daily Bread

In a short space, St. Ambrose sums up the arguments for attending Mass every day of every week. It all starts with the Lord's Prayer and the petition for "our daily bread." The Church Fathers overwhelmingly interpreted this petition in light of the Eucharist.

"Give us this day our daily bread."

When the words of Christ have been uttered, it is no longer called bread, but is named "body." Why then, in the Lord's Prayer, does He say "bread"?

Indeed, He did call it bread, but He called it *epiousion,* which is Greek for "supersubstantial." So it is not bread that passes into the body. It is, rather, the "bread of eternal life" (see Jn 6:35-58), which supports the substance of our soul.

The Latin, however, calls this bread "daily." But if it is "daily" bread, then why do you take it so infrequently? Take daily what will help you daily. And live so that you deserve to receive it daily. He who does not deserve to receive it daily, does not deserve to receive it once a year. Holy Job offered sacrifice daily for his sons, just in case they had sinned in heart or word (see Jb 1:5).

As often as the sacrifice is offered, the Lord's death, the Lord's resurrection, the Lord's ascension, and the remission of sins are signified — and still you don't take this bread of life daily? He who has a wound needs a medicine. The wound is that we are under sin; the medicine is the heavenly and venerable sacrament.

"Give us this day our daily bread." If you receive daily, daily is today for you.

Take It to Prayer

If it is "daily" bread, then why do you take it so infrequently? Take daily what will help you daily.

The bread of eternal life supports the substance of our soul.

He who has a wound needs a medicine. The wound is sin; the medicine is the heavenly sacrament.

Learn It by Heart

Live so that you deserve to receive Christ daily.

Apply It to Your Life

Examine your schedule, examine your priorities, and ask yourself whether you should go to Mass more often than you do.

WEEK 5

with St. Augustine of Hippo

On the Church

St. Augustine (354-430) is one of the pivotal figures in the history of the world. As the old order of the Roman Empire was crumbling, St. Augustine took its noblest ideas and worked them into a bold synthesis for the future. It would be his vision that inspired philosophers and theologians, churchmen and statesmen through the centuries that followed the empire's demise.

St. Augustine was the most brilliant thinker of his day, and we feel his influence down to our own. It is fair to say that he established autobiography as a literary genre. He made important contributions to many other fields, from political philosophy to biblical interpretation. He remains the most influential theologian in the history of the West, and his work is cited in official Church documents more often than that of any other writer outside the Bible.

Augustine's family lived in Tagaste, North Africa (modern Algeria). His father, Patricius, was a pagan Roman official, a rough man and a philanderer. His mother, Monica, was a devout woman. Unfortunately, in his early life, Augustine followed in the ways of his father.

While ill as a teenager, Augustine committed himself to Christ and said he intended to be baptized. But on recovering, he forgot about his recent fervor. He deferred baptism and preferred, instead, a life given over to worldly ambition and pleasures of the flesh.

At sixteen, he left home to study in the city of Carthage. He soon took a mistress, and the couple had a son out of wedlock.

Augustine advanced in the study of rhetoric and held a particular fascination for philosophy. He was obsessed with the problem of evil; in search of a solution, he dabbled in the fashionable pagan mysticism of his day. He took a guru, but could never quite convince himself of those strange doctrines from the Far East. His mother, deeply troubled by all this, prayed intensely for her son.

As a professor of rhetoric, Augustine was a prodigy, and he advanced rapidly to prestigious positions. He won awards for his poetry. He belonged with the world's finest, and so he determined to move to the world's capital, to Rome.

Restless, however, he detoured to Milan, where he was soon joined by his mother. It was she who introduced him to St. Ambrose, and it was Ambrose who persuaded the brilliant young man of the truth of the Scriptures.

Augustine received instruction from the bishop of Milan, and received the sacraments from his hands.

With his now-widowed mother, his now-teenaged son, and several longtime friends, Augustine retired to a semi-monastic life of prayer and study. The companions decided to return to North Africa, and, along the way, Monica died a holy death.

Back in Africa, Augustine received the sacrament of holy orders, and soon after that received the fullness of the sacrament, as he was ordained a bishop. Through almost three decades, he wrote pastoral and theological works that fill many dozens of volumes. He corresponded with Christians everywhere who sought his sage advice. And he preached many times each week. It is likely that he delivered several thousand homilies while bishop. But his greatest homilies are arguably those in which he revealed the mysteries to newly baptized Christians. These he composed with a virtuosity that surpassed that of his old master, St. Ambrose.

Augustine taught that God "wrote" the world the way people write words. Our words are signs of things. Well, God's words, too, are signs of things — but even His things are signs. They are signs of even greater realities. Thus, Moses' passing through the Red Sea was a real historical event, but it was also a sign that prefigured the sacrament of baptism. Jesus' own life was a real human life; yet it was also a sign of the inner life of God through all eternity: the life-giving love that characterizes the Blessed Trinity.

In the same way, the sacraments are sensible realities; but they are also visible signs of invisible mysteries. In every Mass, the priest's consecration changes the bread and wine to the body and blood of Christ. Augustine speaks of the sacrament in uncompromisingly realistic terms. Yet the appearances of the sacrament are also signs of the invisible bond of unity in the Church.

Augustine's sacramental metaphors are not original. Most of them come from St. Paul's letters. But Augustine imbues them with an eloquence and a warmth that are entirely his own. Throughout his life, he was famous for his ability to win

friends. Historians say that at least three major heresies and
two major schisms ended because Augustine won over the
wayward Christians through kindness and persuasion. His
sermons ring with friendship — for us who hear him —
even these many centuries after his death.

29

St. Augustine of Hippo

Reading the Signs

Scholars often remark on the "realism" of St. Augustine's doctrine of the sacraments. He teaches very clearly that in the Mass, the bread and wine undergo a change in their substance and become something else entirely. Yet even the sacrament stands as a sign of something more: the mystery in all its glory. In the sacrament of the altar, Jesus is as really present as He will be at the end of history, when He comes to judge the world. But now He is hidden; then He will be revealed to our sight. Here, St. Augustine discusses the eucharistic bread as the reality of Christ's body, but also as a sign of the unity of the Church, which is Christ's body on earth.

What you see on the altar, you saw last night. But what it was, what it meant, what a great thing the sacrament contained you had not heard. What you see is bread and a chalice. That's what your eyes tell you. But your faith demands instruction.

The bread is Christ's body; the chalice, Christ's blood. It's said briefly, and maybe that's enough for faith. But faith desires understanding. So said the prophet: "If you will not believe, surely you shall not understand" (Is 7:9, Septuagint). Now you can say to me, "You've told us to believe. Now explain so that we can understand it." For such thoughts can come to mind: "We know where Our Lord Jesus Christ took flesh: of the Virgin Mary. As a baby He was nursed, nourished, grew, and reached the stage of young manhood. He suffered persecution and was hanged on a tree; He was taken down from the tree, buried, and on the third day He rose again, on the day He wished for, and He ascended into heaven. He lifted His body to heaven, and from heaven He will come to judge the living and the dead. There He sits at the right hand of the Father. So how is this bread His body? And how can the cup — or what fills the cup — be His blood?"

These are called sacraments, brothers and sisters, because one thing is seen in them while another thing is understood. What you see has a material form; what you understand is its spiritual fruit.

So if you want to understand the body of Christ, listen to what the apostle tells the faithful: "Now you are the body of Christ and individually members of it" (1 Cor 12:27). If you are the body of Christ and its members, you are the mystery that has been placed on the Lord's table, and you are the mystery that you receive! You respond "Amen" to what you are, and in responding you agree. You hear "the body of Christ," and you respond, "Amen." Then be a member of the body of Christ, so that your Amen may be true.

Why then in bread? Let's say nothing on our own here, but listen instead to what the apostle says when he speaks of the sacrament: "Because there is one bread, we who are many are one body, for we all partake of the one bread" (1 Cor 10:17).

Ponder and rejoice! Unity, truth, piety, charity — one bread! And what is this one bread? "We who are many are one body!" Remember that bread is not made from a single grain of wheat, but from many. When you were exorcised, it was like a grinding. When you were baptized, it was like being mixed into dough. When you received the fire of the Holy Spirit, it was like being baked. So be what you can see, and become what you are.

That's what the apostle said about the bread. What we are to understand about the chalice is clear, even if it is left unsaid. For just as many grains come together to produce the visible form of bread, so it is that the Scripture says of the faithful: "Now the company of those who believed were of one heart and soul" (Acts 4:32). And so it's the same with the wine. Remember, brothers and sisters, how wine is made. Many grapes hang in the cluster, but the juice of the grapes flows together in one liquid.

That is how Christ the Lord signified us, and how He wished us to belong to Him. That is how He consecrated the mystery of our peace and unity on His table. Whoever accepts the mystery of unity but does not hold the bond of peace, does not receive it for his own good, but rather as a testimony against himself.

Take It to Prayer

~~≈≈~~

Faith demands instruction. Faith desires understanding.

These are called sacraments because one thing is seen in them while another thing is understood. What you see has a material form; what you understand is its spiritual fruit.

Why then in bread? Remember that bread is not made from a single grain of wheat, but from many. So be what you can see, and become what you are.

Learn It by Heart

~~≈≈~~

If you are the body of Christ and its members, you are the mystery placed on the Lord's table, and you are the mystery you receive!

Apply It to Your Life

~~≈≈~~

The spiritual mystery at the heart of the Eucharist is rich indeed: It is the unity of the Church; it is the bond of charity, which is the inner life of the Trinity; it is peace. When we receive Communion, we pledge ourselves to the cause of unity, charity, peace in the soul, and peace on earth. Unity, charity, peace: When we violate these, especially in our speech, we bear testimony against ourselves. Today, pay special attention to the way you speak about others — their actions, their motives, even their looks. Watch for the patterns of sarcasm, irony, or exaggeration that spread, like rot through wheat, and keep us from becoming what we are.

30

St. Augustine of Hippo

The Process of Conversion

The sacraments are flesh-and-blood realities; they are divine realities. Yet they are also rich in their symbolic value. St. Augustine shows that the rites of Christian initiation correspond, at every stage, to the process of making bread and wine — from the harvesting of wheat and grapes through the grinding and the crushing, baking, and fermenting.

Because the Lord suffered for us, He left us His body and blood in this sacrament, which He made from us ourselves as well. For we are made into His body, and through His mercy we are what we receive.

Recall that once you did not exist; you have been created. You were brought to the Lord's threshing floor, and threshed by the work of oxen; that is, by those who preach the Gospel. When you were catechumens, you were temporarily kept under observation in the granary. Then you were named on the list. Then began the process of grinding, through fasts and exorcisms. Afterward, you came to the water: You were sprinkled, and you all were made into one dough. You were baked by the heat of the Holy Spirit, and you became the Lord's bread.

Consider what you have received! Just as you see the bread made one, so may you also be one body — by loving one another, by having one faith, one hope, and an undivided charity. When heretics receive this, they receive testimony against themselves, because they seek division, while this bread bespeaks unity. So, too, the wine was formerly in many clusters of grapes; and now it is one. It is one in the beautiful golden chalice, after the crushing of the winepress. And now you — after the fasts, after the labors, after the humiliations and contrition — have come, in the name of Christ, to the Lord's own chalice.

And there you are on the table! And there you are in the chalice! You are one with us. We receive together, we drink together, because we live together.

Take It to Prayer

You became the Lord's bread.

Be one body — by loving one another, by having one faith, one hope, and an undivided charity.

We receive together, we drink together, because we live together.

Learn It by Heart

~≫e❦ে~

We are made into His body, and through His mercy we are what we receive.

Apply It to Your Life

~≫e❦ে~

Look back on the process of conversion that has brought you closer to Jesus Christ. Make a list of the major milestones along the way. If you feel so moved, briefly write out your story — addressing it to God in thanksgiving, as St. Augustine did.

31

St. Augustine of Hippo

Identification Check

St. Paul often spoke of the Church as Christ's body. For St. Augustine, this was more than a metaphor. It implied an entire theology of the sacraments, of prayer, and of everyday joy and suffering.

"He put a new song in my mouth" (Ps 40:3).

If anyone should ask who is speaking in this Psalm, I would say, in a word, "It is Christ."

But as you know, brothers and sisters — and as we must often say — Christ sometimes speaks in the name of our Head; and sometimes He speaks of us who are His members. For when He said, "I was hungry and you gave me food" (Mt 25:35), He spoke on behalf of His members, not Himself. And when He said, "Saul, Saul, why do you persecute me?" (Acts 9:4), the Head cried out on behalf of its members. Yet He did not say, "Why do you persecute my members?" He said, "Why do you persecute me?"

If He suffers in us, then we shall be crowned in Him. Such is the love of Christ. What can be compared to this? This is the reason He says, "He put a new song in my mouth, a song of praise to our God." He speaks on behalf of His members.

"A body hast thou prepared for me" (Heb 10:5). We are in this body. We are partakers of this body. We know what we ourselves receive. A body has been perfected for us; let us be perfected in the body.

We have the body of Christ. We have the blood of Christ. If we have a new life, let us sing "a new song ... a song of praise to our God."

Take It to Prayer

A body has been perfected for us; let us be perfected in the body.

If He suffers in us, then we shall be crowned in Him.

If we have a new life, let us sing a song of praise to our God.

Learn It by Heart

What can be compared to the love of Christ?

Apply It to Your Life

All love seeks closer union. God so loved us that He become one with us, and He became one of us. He identified Himself with His Church in every place and every age, and He made of us one bread and one body. Our sufferings are His. Our joys are his. Are His sufferings ours as well? Are His joys our joys? Do we suffer and rejoice as Jesus did when He walked among us on earth?

32

St. Augustine of Hippo

To Him, Through Him, In Him

St. Augustine discusses the great mystery of our conversation with God: Christ is the subject of our prayer and the object of our prayer, so close is His union with us.

No greater gift could God have given us than to make His Word, by which He created all things, our Head, joining us to Him as His members, so that the Son of God might become the Son of Man — one God with the Father, one man with us.

So when we speak to God in prayer for mercy, we do not separate the Son from Him; and when the body of the Son prays, it does not separate its head from itself. It is one Savior of His body, our Lord Jesus Christ, the Son of God, who prays for us, and prays in us, and is prayed to by us. He prays for us as our priest. He prays in us as our head. He is prayed to by us as our God. Let us therefore recognize our words in Him, and His words in us. He is prayed to in the form of God. In the form of a servant He prays. There the Creator, here the created — the unchanged assuming a creaturely form in order to change it, and making us with Himself one man, head and body.

So we pray to Him, through Him, in Him. And we speak with Him, and He speaks with us. We speak in Him, He speaks in us the prayer of this Psalm (86), which is titled, "A Prayer of David." For our Lord was son of David, according to the flesh; but according to His divine nature, He was the Lord of David, and his Maker.... Let no one, then, on hearing these words, say "It is not Christ who speaks," or say "It is not I who speaks." No, rather, if he considers himself to be in the body of Christ, let him say "Both Christ speaks and I speak." You should be unwilling to say anything without Him, and He says nothing without you.

Take It to Prayer

It is one Christ who prays for us, and prays in us, and is prayed to by us.

He is prayed to in the form of God. In the form of a servant He prays.

You should be unwilling to say anything without Christ, and He says nothing without you.

Learn It by Heart

The Son of God became the Son of Man — one God with the Father, one man with us.

Apply It to Your Life

Set time aside for prayer and stay faithful to your time of prayer. We are Christ's body, and He prays in us, even if we don't feel like praying on a particular day. God does not ask us for sparkling eloquence or intense emotion, just fidelity.

33

St. Augustine of Hippo

Scandals and Sinners in the Church

St. Augustine acknowledges that the Church is always beset by scandals and sinners. That is exactly as Jesus predicted it would be. Yet believers must never leave the Church on account of its sinners. Once again, St. Augustine gives a mystagogical explanation of the Church as Christ's eucharistic bread, and the believers as individual grains of wheat. The wheat must not try to separate itself from the chaff by leaving the threshing floor. For it is to the threshing floor that Christ will come to gather His wheat.

In the book called Genesis, Scripture says: "And God saw that the light was good; and God separated the light from the darkness. God called the light Day, and the darkness he called Night" (Gen 1:4-5). The Lord called the light Day, and undoubtedly those to whom the apostle Paul says, "for once you were darkness, but now you are light in the Lord" (Eph 5:8) were the Day, because He who commanded light to shine out of darkness has illumined them (see 2 Cor 4:6).

Those "infants" whom you see outwardly dressed in white and inwardly cleansed — whose radiant garments bespeak the splendor of their souls — they were once the darkness, overshadowed by the night of their sins. But now

189

they have been washed in the bath of indulgence, watered by the fount of wisdom, and soaked with the light of justice: "This is the day which the LORD has made; let us rejoice and be glad in it" (Ps 118:24). Let the Lord's Day hear us! Let the Day made by the Lord hear us! Let it hear and listen, so that we may rejoice and be glad in it. As the apostle says, this is our "joy and crown" if you "stand firm thus in the Lord" (Phil 4:1).

So listen to us, O newborns of a chaste mother. Listen, you children of a virgin mother. Because "you were darkness, but now you are light in the Lord, walk as children of light" (Eph 5:8) and stay close to the children of light. Let me speak plainly here: Stay close to the faithful who are good. Because there are, sad to say, believers who are evil. There are some who are called believers, though they are not. There are believers who abuse the sacraments of Christ, people who live in such a way that they themselves perish while they destroy others. They perish from their evil way of living; they destroy others by the example of their wicked lives. Do not join them, dearly beloved. Seek the good; cling to the good; be good.

Don't be surprised at the multitude of bad Christians who fill the church, who go up to the altar for Communion, who make a big deal of praising the bishop or priest when he speaks about good morals. Such people fulfill the prediction made by our shepherd in the psalm: "Were I to proclaim and tell of them, they would be more than can be numbered" (Ps 40:5). They can be with us in the Church of this time, but, after the resurrection, they will be unable to remain in the congregation of saints. The Church of this time has good mixed with bad. It is like a threshing floor, where grain is mixed with chaff, good members mixed together with evil. But, after the judgment, it will have all good members, without the evil. This threshing floor holds the harvest planted by the apostles and watered in turn by good teachers down to the present time. It has been threshed a bit by the persecution of enemies; now only the purification of the final winnowing remains to be done. And indeed He is coming, of whom you have repeated in the creed: "He will come to judge the living and the dead." As the Gospel says: "His winnowing fork is in his hand, to clear His threshing floor, and to gather the wheat into his granary, but the chaff he will burn with unquenchable fire" (Lk 3:17).

You older faithful people should also hear what I say: May the grain rejoice with trembling, and remain, and not leave the threshing floor. May you never try, by your own judgment, to free yourself from the chaff; for you cannot remain on the threshing floor if you seek to separate yourself now from the chaff. What's more, when Christ comes — He Who judges without error — He will not raise to the granary anything He has not found on the threshing floor. And those grains that have left the threshing floor will boast in vain about where they came from. The granary will be filled and closed. Fire will consume whatever is left outside.

So, brothers and sisters, those who are good must put up with evil. Those who are bad must imitate the good. On this threshing floor, grain can rot into chaff, and grain can rise up from the chaff. Such changes take place every day, my brothers and sisters. This life is full of humiliations and consolations. Every day, seemingly good people do wrong and die; yet seemingly evil people are converted and live. For God takes no "pleasure in the death of the wicked," but only "that he should turn from his way and live" (Ezek 18:23).

Listen to me, grains of wheat! Listen, you who are what I wish you to be! Don't be saddened by the mixture with chaff. The evil ones will not be with you forever. How heavy, after all, is that pile of husks? It's light, thank God! We must only remain as grains and then, however heavy it gets, it will not crush us. "God is faithful, and He will not let you be tempted beyond your strength, but with the temptation will also provide the way of escape, that you may be able to endure it" (1 Cor 10:13).

Let the chaff also listen! Let them listen, wherever they are. I do not wish chaff to be here; but, if they are, let's urge them. Listen, then, O chaff; although, if you do listen, you will no longer be chaff. Listen, then. May God's patience help you; may the close company of the grain and may these words of advice make you, too, into grain. You do not lack the rainshowers of the words of God. Don't let the field in you be barren. So come to life again! Grow grain and ripen! For He who planted you wishes to find full ears of wheat, not thorns.

Take It to Prayer

Stay close to the faithful who are good. Seek the good; cling to the good; be good.

The Church of this time has good members mixed together with evil. But, after the judgment, it will have all good members, without the evil.

Every day, seemingly good people do wrong and die; yet seemingly evil people are converted and live.

Learn It by Heart

Never try, by your own judgment, to free yourself from the chaff; for you cannot remain on the threshing floor if you seek to separate yourself now from the chaff.

Apply It to Your Life

Do not be downhearted because of scandals in the Church. Jesus Himself warned that scandals would come, and that the wicked would be judged and punished. We should rest in His promise. We should rest in His one true Church, even if within the Church we find much unrest.

34

St. Augustine of Hippo

The Church Is the Kingdom

*Sacraments are signs of deeper mysteries. But their earthly quali-
ties can also deceive us. We can rely so much on the data of our
senses that we doubt the spiritual realities that are invisible. The
Catholic Church, says St. Augustine, is the kingdom of Christ,
right here, right now. There is no other way to read Jesus' parables,
which describe not a kingdom purified, but a place full of goodness mixed with wickedness. The Catholic Church is the kingdom,
and this is true in spite of the great number of scandalous sinners
who publicly profess the faith. Appearances do not tell the whole
story. For that, we must await the return of Jesus Christ, when the
kingdom will come in its fullness. Now it is concealed in mystery;
then it will be revealed in glory.*

While the devil is bound, the saints reign with Christ during the time between His first and second coming. For
the Church could not now be called His kingdom or "the
kingdom of heaven" unless His saints were even now reigning
with Him; for to His saints He says, "I am with you always, to
the close of the age" (Mt 28:20). Surely it is in this present time
that the scribe trained for the kingdom of God brings forth
from his treasure things new and old (see Mt 13:52). And it is

from the Church that the reapers shall gather the tares that He allowed to grow alongside the wheat until the harvest, as He explains: "The harvest is the close of the age, and the reapers are angels. Just as the weeds are gathered and burned with fire, so will it be at the close of the age. The Son of man will send His angels, and they will gather out of His kingdom all causes of sin and all evildoers" (Mt 13:39-41). Can He mean that they are gathered out of the future kingdom in which there are no offenses? Of course not. Then they must be gathered out of His present kingdom, the Church.

We must understand, on the one hand, the kingdom of heaven in which those who break His teaching coexist with those who do His teaching. The one is the least, and the other the great. On the other hand, we must also understand the kingdom of heaven into which only the doer of Christ's teaching shall enter. Where both classes exist, it is the Church as it now is. But where only the one shall exist, it is the Church as it is destined to be, when no wicked person shall remain in her.

So the Church even now is the kingdom of Christ and the kingdom of heaven. Even now His saints reign with Him, though in a different way than they will reign in the hereafter. And, though the tares grow alongside the wheat in the Church, they do not reign with Him. For those who reign with Him are those who do as the apostle says: "If then you have been raised with Christ, seek the things that are above, where Christ is, seated at the right hand of God. Set your minds on things that are above, not on things that are on earth" (Col 3:1-2). Of such people he also says that their "commonwealth is in heaven" (Phi 3:20). In short, they reign with Him who are so in His kingdom that they themselves *are* His kingdom.

But what about those who are in it until all evildoers are gathered out at the end of the world? What about those who seek their own things, and not the things that are Christ's? In what sense are they the kingdom of Christ?

We all live in this kingdom militant — amid conflict with the enemy, waging war against our rebellious desires, and governing them as they yield — until we come to that most peaceful kingdom where we shall reign without an enemy. And it is of this first resurrection, in the present life, that the Book of Revelation speaks when it says that the devil is bound a thousand years and is afterward loosed for a short season (see Rev 20:2-6). It goes on to sketch out what the Church does, and what is done in the Church, in those days: "Then I saw thrones, and seated on them were those to whom judgment was committed" (Rev 20:4). Don't think that this refers to the last judgment. It refers, rather, to the rulers by whom the Church is now governed and the thrones from which they rule. And no better interpretation of judgment being given can be produced than the words, "Whatever you bind on earth shall be bound in heaven, and whatever you loose on earth shall be loosed in heaven" (Mt 18:18). So the apostle says, "For what have I to do with judging outsiders? Is it not those inside the Church whom you are to judge?" (1 Cor 5:12).

And, says John, "the souls of those who had been beheaded for their testimony to Jesus and for the word of God ... reigned with Christ a thousand years" (Rev 20:4). These are the souls of the martyrs not yet restored to their bodies. For the souls of the pious dead are not separated from the Church, which even now is the kingdom of Christ. Otherwise there would be no remembrance of them at the altar of God in the partaking of the body of Christ. Nor would it do any good in danger to run to baptism, so that we might not pass from this life without it; nor to the sacrament of reconciliation, if by impenitence or a bad conscience any one may be severed from His body. For why are these things practiced, if not because the faithful, even though dead, are His members?

So, while these "thousand years" run on, their souls reign with Him, though not yet joined with their bodies. And therefore in another part of this same book we read, "Blessed are the dead who die in the Lord henceforth. 'Blessed indeed,' says the Spirit, 'that they may rest from their labors, for their deeds follow them'" (Rev 14:13).

The Church, then, begins its reign now, with Christ, in the living and the dead. For, as the apostle says: "To this end Christ died and lived again, that he might be Lord both of the dead and of the living" (Rom 14:9). He mentioned the souls of the martyrs only, because they have contended for the truth, even to the point of death, and their reign is most glorious after death. But we should take the part for the whole and understand this passage to include all others who belong to the Church, which is the kingdom of Christ.

Take It to Prayer

The Church even now is the kingdom of Christ and the kingdom of heaven. Even now His saints reign with Him, though in a different way than they will reign in the here-after.

They reign with Him who are so in His kingdom that they themselves are His kingdom.

The souls of the pious dead are not separated from the Church. Otherwise there would be no remembrance of them in the Mass.

Learn It by Heart

The Church begins its reign now, with Christ, in the living and the dead.

Apply It to Your Life

St. Augustine shows us a panorama of the whole Church, whose fellowship we should know at every level. There is the Church militant, made up of those who still struggle on earth. There is the Church suffering, made up of the souls in purgatory, whom we remember at Mass and in our prayers. And there is the Church triumphant, made up of the saints in heaven. We should live a deep friendship with our entire spiritual family, never forgetting the dead, never mistaking any part for the whole. We need to show charity toward our brothers and sisters still here on earth; we need to pray daily for the souls in purgatory; and we need to ask the intercession, and follow the example, of the saints in heaven.

35

St. Augustine of Hippo

The Mystery of the Mass

In this sermon, St. Augustine brings together all the major themes of his mystagogy: the theology of signs; the flesh-and-blood realism; the power of the consecration; the Church as Christ's mystical body; the identification of the Christian with Christ.

I haven't forgotten my promise. I promised you, who are newly baptized, a sermon explaining the sacrament of the Lord's table, which you now look upon and which you shared last night. You ought to know what you have received, what you are going to receive, and what you should receive every day. That bread you see on the altar, made holy by the Word of God, is the body of Christ. That chalice — or rather, what fills the chalice, made holy by the Word of God — is the blood of Christ.

Through those appearances the Lord wished to leave us His body and the blood that He poured out for the remission of sins. If you receive well, you are what you have received. The apostle says: "We who are many are one body, for we all partake of the one bread" (1 Cor 10:17). Thus he explained the sacrament of the Lord's table: "Because there is one bread, we who are many are one body." So it is bread that teaches you how you should love unity. Was that bread made from one grain of wheat? Weren't there many grains? Yet before they became bread, they were separate. After some crushing, they were joined together by water. For unless the grain is ground up and moistened with water, it cannot come to that form called bread.

You, too, were once ground up, so to speak, by the humiliation of fasting and by the sacrament of exorcism. Then followed the baptism of water. You were moistened, so to speak, so as to come to the form of bread. But there is no bread without fire. What does the fire signify? It's the chrism. The oil of the sacrament of the Holy Spirit, the sacrament of confirmation, is what feeds our fire. Notice this when the Acts of the Apostles are read aloud. So anyone who wants to move forward has what it takes.

When you assemble in church, leave aside empty stories. Concentrate on the Scriptures. So listen and watch; for the Holy Spirit will come at Pentecost. And this is how He comes: In tongues of fire He will show Himself. He breathes charity into us, which gives us ardor for God and contempt for the world; it burns up our chaff and purifies our hearts like gold.

So the fire of the Holy Spirit comes after the water. Then you become bread, which is the body of Christ. And that is how unity is signified.

Now you have the sacraments in their order. First, after the prayer, you are urged to "Lift up your hearts!" This is only right, because you are members of Christ. If you have become members of Christ, where is your Head? Members have a head. If the Head had not gone before, the members wouldn't follow. And where has your Head gone? What did you say in the creed? "On the third day He rose again from the dead. He ascended into heaven. He sits at the right hand of the Father." Our Head is in heaven! So to "Lift up your hearts," you answer, "We lift them up to the Lord." You must not attribute this to your own strength, your merits, or your works; for to lift up our hearts to God is itself a gift from God, and that is why, after the answer "We lift them up to the Lord," the bishop or priest who is presiding says, "Let us give thanks to the Lord our God." Let us give thanks because without His help, we would have our hearts on earth. And you attest to this by saying: "It is right to give Him thanks and praise" — Him, Who made us able to lift up our hearts to our Head.

Then comes the sanctification of God's sacrifice; for He wanted us ourselves to be His sacrifice, a fact made clear when the sacrifice was first offered, and because the sacrifice is a sign of what we are. After the consecration, we say the Lord's Prayer, which you have received and recited. Afterward it is said: "Peace be with you." And Christians greet one another with a holy kiss. This is a sign of peace. As the lips show forth, so may it be in the conscience. As your lips approach those of your brother or sister, your heart should not be far away.

These are great and mighty sacraments! Do you want to know how they are commended to us? The apostle says:

"Whoever, therefore, eats the bread or drinks the cup of the Lord in an unworthy manner will be guilty of profaning the body and blood of the Lord" (1 Cor 11:27). What is receiving unworthily? To receive as a joke, to receive in contempt. Don't belittle the sacrament just because you can look upon it. What you see passes away; but the invisible, the thing that is signified, does not pass away, but remains.

Look: It's received, eaten, consumed. But is Christ's body consumed? Is Christ's Church consumed? Are Christ's members consumed? No. Here they are cleansed; there they will be crowned. What is signified will last forever, even though the sign seems to pass away.

Receive so that you may reflect, that you all may hold unity close in your hearts, that you may always "Lift up your hearts." Let your hope be in heaven, and not on earth. Let your faith be firm in God. Let it be acceptable to God. Now you do not see, but you believe. There you will see, in the place where you will have endless joy.

Take It to Prayer

You ought to know what you have received, what you are going to receive, and what you should receive every day.

If you receive well, you are what you have received.

He wanted us ourselves to be His sacrifice, because the sacrifice is a sign of what we are.

Learn It by Heart

～え9～

What is signified will last forever, even though the sign seems to pass away.

Apply It to Your Life

～え9～

St. Augustine urges us to go to Mass every day, if possible. We should long for Jesus, the bread come down from heaven. But even when we cannot get to Mass, we should tell Him of our longing. This traditional practice is called a prayer of "spiritual communion." If we tell Jesus we want to receive Him devoutly, He will give us the grace of communion with Him.

WEEK 6

with St. John Chrysostom

Ways of Life

Chrysostom is not a name John received from his parents. It was the name he earned from the congregations who loved him. Chrysostomos means "Golden Mouth" in Greek.

John (349-407) was the son of a very prominent and wealthy imperial official in Antioch, Syria, one of the great Christian cities in the ancient Church. John never knew his father, however, as the man died while his only child was still an infant. John's mother, Anthousa, was just twenty years old when she was widowed. But she resolved to follow the biblical counsel that it is well for widows to remain single (see 1 Cor 7:8). She gave herself completely to John's upbringing and education. She arranged for him to study under the world's most famous professor of rhetoric, the pagan Libanios. Indeed, John became his star pupil.

At eighteen, however, John's interests turned to "divine learning." He enlisted himself for baptism and placed himself under the tutelage of the renowned Scripture scholar Diodore of Tarsus. Soon, once again, John was the most brilliant pupil of his master.

In early adulthood, John remained with his mother, who noticed his strict fasting and feared he would enter a monastery, leaving her a widow again. John deferred to her wishes until he could no longer resist God's call. He went off into a mountain cave, where he lived a hermit's life for two years.

When John returned to the city, his bishop ordained him first as a deacon and then as a priest. For twelve years, he was the main preacher in the city's cathedral church. There, he preached the homilies that earned him his fame.

It was his fame as a preacher that brought him to the attention of the wider Church, and especially the imperial court. When the patriarch of Constantinople died, the emperor unexpectedly summoned John from Antioch to the most powerful bishop's throne in the East. John declined the honor. But the emperor ordered him to be taken by force, and so he was.

An imperial city is a hotbed of envy, flattery, political maneuvering, and precipitously rising and falling fortunes. John's habitual honesty and integrity did not serve him well, by capital standards. He was a reformer and an ascetic, demanding much of others but even more of himself. The clergy of Constantinople were not, however, eager to be reformed or to imitate John's spartan lifestyle. Nor was the imperial family, especially the empress, interested in John's advice about their cosmetics, their lavish expenses, and their self-aggrandizing monuments. John found it outrageous that the rich could relieve themselves in golden chamber pots while the poor went hungry.

Ordinary people found inspiration, solace, and — no doubt — entertainment in the great man's preaching. But the powerful were not amused. They arranged a kangaroo court of bishops to depose John in 403. In fact, a military unit interrupted the liturgy during the Easter Vigil, just as John was preparing to baptize a group of catechumens. Historians record that the baptismal waters ran red with blood.

John was sent away to the wild country on the eastern end of the Black Sea. Yet even there he attracted disciples. This further infuriated the imperial authorities, who wanted John silenced permanently.

John's health was never good, and his guards took advantage of this. In moving him to a new location, they forced him to go on foot. They marched him to death on September 14, 407.

Soon after taking the imperial throne, the son of the empress who ordered John's death recalled John's body to an honored grave in the capital city.

John's homilies are rich in mystagogical content. For this book, we chose his most powerful material on the sacraments of marriage and holy orders. When we live these sacraments well, we live as signs of deeper mysteries — of divine life.

36

St. John Chrysostom

The Two Become One Flesh

St. John shows that the bodily union of man and wife is an image of the spiritual union of Christ and the Church.

What, then? Is marriage a theater? No! It is a mystery and a symbol of something mighty. Even if you don't show it honor, then honor what it symbolizes. "This mystery," says St. Paul, "is a profound one, and I am saying that it refers to Christ and the church" (Eph 5:32).

It is a symbol of the Church, and of Christ. The two come together, and they make one. When two come together, they do not make a lifeless image, or the image of anything on earth, but of God Himself. Two come to marriage, about to be made one body. See again a mystery of love! If the two do not become one — if they remain two — they do not make many. But when they unite, then they make many.

What do we learn from this? That the power of union is mighty. The wisdom of God, in the beginning, divided the one in two; but He wanted to show that it remained one even after division. So He made it impossible for either alone to be enough for procreation. For neither can be one until united with the other. Each is only half. Each alone can produce no children.

Do you see the mystery of marriage? He made one from one; and after He made these two into one, He made one, so that now, also, children are produced from one. For husband and wife are not two, but one. This may be confirmed from many sources; for instance, from the words "male and female He created them" (Gen 1:27). If he is the head and she the body, how are they two? From the very fashioning of the body, one may see that they are one, for she was made from his side, and they are two halves.

And how do they become one flesh? As if she were pure gold receiving pure gold, so the woman receives the man's seed. She nourishes it and cherishes it and adds her own share, the two fused by pleasure. And so she gives it back as a child!

The child is a sort of bridge, so that the three become one flesh, the child connecting, on either side, each to the other. Two cities, though divided by a river, become one if a bridge connects them. How much more, then, if the very bridge is formed of the substance of each.

Why are you blushing? Leave that to the heretics and pagans, with their impure and immodest customs. For this reason I want marriage to be thoroughly purified, to bring it back again to its proper nobility. You should not be ashamed of these things; if you are ashamed, then you condemn God who made marriage.

So I shall tell you how marriage is a mystery of the Church. The Church was made from Christ's side, and He united with her in a spiritual union. For one man said: "I betrothed you to Christ to present you as a pure bride to her one husband" (2 Cor. 11:2). And he goes on to say that "we are members of His body" (Eph 5:30).

Think about all these things, then, and let's not cast shame upon so great a mystery. Marriage is a symbol of the presence of Christ. Tell me: If you saw an image of the king, would you dishonor it? By no means.

Take It to Prayer

Marriage is a mystery and a symbol of something mighty. It is a symbol of the Church, and of Christ.

For this reason I want marriage to be thoroughly purified, to bring it back again to its proper nobility.

Two come together, and they make one, an image of God Himself. See again a mystery of love! If the two do not become one — if they remain two — they do not make many. But when they unite, then they make many.

Learn It by Heart

Marriage is a symbol of the presence of Christ.

Apply It to Your Life

Catholic teaching on marriage and sex is not just a list of rules and prohibitions. It is an expression of the deepest mysteries of God, Christ, and the Church. Christ's love for the Church is always fruitful and life-giving. That is why, for example, the Church forbids the use of artificial contraceptives. To sin against God's design for human sexuality is to "dishonor the image of the king," Jesus Christ. Strive to acquire a mature understanding of Catholic teaching on marriage and sexual morality, as it is expressed in the official documents of the Church.

37

St. John Chrysostom

The Secret to Lasting Love

*St. John knew what made for happy homes: in a word, sacrifice.
Spouses would never know happiness as long as they practiced
coercion, selfishness, and domination. The best way to rule is by
serving. There is neither love nor joy in a household held together
by threats and terror. The truly orderly home is an image of Christ's
mystical marriage to the Church; its hallmarks are enduring
"thoughtfulness, affection, kindness."*

"Husbands," St. Paul said, "love your wives, as Christ loved
the Church" (Eph 5:25).

Do you want your wife to obey you, as the Church obeys
Christ? Then give her the same care as Christ gives the
Church. Do not refuse any suffering, even if you need to give
your life for her and be cut into pieces ten thousand times.
Even if you undergo all this, still you will not have done
anything like Christ has done. For you are doing it for someone to whom you are already joined; but He did it for someone who turned her back on Him and hated Him.

He didn't threaten her with violence or terror. No, He
gave His unwearied affection to her, who turned her back on
Him — who hated Him, rejected Him, and showed Him

217

disrespect. You should behave the same way toward your spouse. Even if, in return, you receive hatred, rejection, and disrespect, still you will succeed by your great thoughtfulness, affection, kindness. For the partner of one's life, the parent of one's children, the foundation of one's every joy should never be chained down by fear and threats, but with love and good temper. What sort of union would that be, where the wife trembles at her husband? And what sort of pleasure will the husband himself enjoy, if he dwells with his wife as with a slave and not a free woman?

Though you should suffer anything on account of your spouse, do not upbraid; for neither did Christ.

"Christ loved the Church and gave himself up for her, that He might sanctify her, having cleansed her" (Eph 5:25-26).

So she was unclean! So she had blemishes, so she was unsightly, so she was worthless! Whatever kind of spouse you take, you'll never have a spouse like the Church was when Christ took her. Nor will you find one so estranged from you as the Church was from Christ. Yet, for all that, He did not hate her for her exceeding ugliness. She was foolish, and she had an evil tongue; and still He gave Himself up for her, as he would for a spouse dearly beloved, young, and beautiful. All this moved Paul to say: "Why, one will hardly die for a righteous man.… But God shows his love for us in that while we were yet sinners Christ died for us" (Rom 5:7-8). Though this was the case, He took her, He arrayed her in beauty, and washed her, and refused not even this, to give Himself for her.

Take It to Prayer

Christ gave His unwearied affection to her who showed Him disrespect.

Do not refuse any suffering, even if you need to give your life for your spouse and be cut into pieces ten thousand times.

Though you should suffer anything on account of your spouse, do not upbraid; for neither did Christ.

Learn It by Heart

The partner of one's life should never be chained down by fear and threats, but with love and good temper.

Apply It to Your Life

When you're at home, make a habit of offering a silent prayer: "I will serve." Then try to serve others by deeds that make life pleasant for them, but perhaps go unnoticed. Expect no gratitude; seek nothing in return but the joy of serving. If you want to tell someone about what you did, tell Jesus.

38

St. John Chrysostom

The Earthly Trinity

Marriage, for St. John, is a living symbol of the mysteries of God. The husband, wife, and child symbolize the Trinity of persons in the godhead. The conjugal union of husband and wife symbolizes the eternal communion of Jesus with the Father. To say that marriage is an allegory or sign of divine love is not to dishonor human love, but indeed to raise it to a greater honor.

"For this reason a man shall leave his father and mother and be joined to his wife, and the two shall become one flesh" (Eph 5:31).

St. Paul shows us that a man leaves the parents who gave him birth and is joined to his wife; and that one flesh — father and mother and child — comes from the combined substance of the two. The child is made from the combination of their seeds, so the three are one flesh.

So are we in relation to Christ: We become one flesh through Communion. We are more united to Him than a child is to his parents.

Don't you see that we have many defects in our own flesh? One man, for example, is lame; another has crippled feet; another withered hands; another has some other disability; and yet he does not begrudge his weaker limb, or cut it off, but treats it more gently than the other, and naturally so, for it is part of himself.

As much love as a man shows himself, so St. Paul would have us show toward a spouse. Not because we share the same nature — no, the duty toward a spouse is far greater than that. It is, rather, because there are not two bodies but one: He is the head, and she is the body. Paul also says that "the head of Christ is God" (1 Cor 11:3). As husband and wife are one body, so also are Christ and the Father one, and the Father is shown to be our Head. Paul sets down two examples, that of the natural body and that of Christ's body. And so he adds: "This mystery is a profound one, and I am saying that it refers to Christ and the church" (Eph 5:32).

Why does he call it a great mystery? Blessed Moses — or rather God — told us in Genesis that it was something great and wonderful. Now, however, Paul speaks about Christ, who left the Father, came down, and came to the Bride, and became one Spirit. "He who is united to the Lord becomes one spirit with Him" (1 Cor 6:17). Paul is right to call this a profound mystery. Then, as if to say, "Still, the allegory does not destroy married love," Paul adds: "However, let each one of you love his wife as himself, and let the wife see that she respects her husband" (Eph 5:33).

A great mystery indeed — and one that holds some hidden wisdom. Moses showed this prophetically in the Book of Genesis; and now Paul, too, proclaims it when he says, "it refers to Christ and the Church."

Take It to Prayer

◦≈⊱≈◦

As husband and wife are one body, so also are Christ and the Father one.

One flesh — father and mother and child — comes from the combined substance of the two. So the three are one flesh.

As much love as a man shows himself, so St. Paul would have us show toward a spouse.

Learn It by Heart

◦≈⊱≈◦

Through Communion we are more united to Christ than a child is to his parents.

Apply It to Your Life

◦≈⊱≈◦

God ordained all life in the human family to reflect the eternal life of the divine family we call the Trinity. All the qualities of a happy home — peace, constancy, charity, providence — abide perfectly in God, who has made us partakers of the divine nature. If we live our sacraments fully and faithfully — marriage, confession, Communion — we just might find our homes grow more heavenly with time.

39

St. John Chrysostom

No Longer Two

Think of the things God has shared with us: His love, His wisdom, His only Son, His very nature. If God has given so much to His children, then we must live our family life in imitation of Him. We must call nothing "mine."

After marriage you are no longer two, but one flesh. Are your possessions, then, divided in two or united as one? You both have become one person, one living creature; and yet you still say "mine"? "Mine" is a cursed and abominable word brought in by the devil. God has taken things far nearer and dearer than these and shared them in common with us — and still we will not share in common? We would never say, "my light," "my sun," "my water." All our greatest blessings are shared in common, and yet not our riches? Death, then, to those riches, ten thousand times over! Or rather not to the riches, but to those tempers of mind that do not know how to make use of riches, but hold them above all things.

Take It to Prayer

Are your possessions divided in two or united as one?

"Mine" is a cursed and abominable word.

Death to all tempers of mind that do not know how to make use of riches.

Learn It by Heart

God has taken things far nearer and dearer than these and shared them in common with us.

Apply It to Your Life

Make a list of the material things whose loss would make you most unhappy. Ask yourself whether your attachment to these things is healthy. Ask yourself whether these things might come between you and God.

40

St. John Chrysostom

Dare to Live Like an Angel

St. John shows how the holiness of celibacy depends upon the holiness of marriage. When marriage loses its place of honor in a culture, the glory of celibacy is lost.

Whoever condemns marriage also deprives celibacy of its glory. But whoever praises marriage makes celibacy more attractive and luminous. Something that seems good only in comparison with something bad is not very good at all. But if it is greater than things that everyone prizes, then indeed it is a most excellent good, as celibacy certainly is.

Is marriage a good thing? Certainly. But then celibacy is more attractive because it is a better thing, as much better as a captain is than his sailors, a general than his soldiers. Even so, if you remove the sailors you halt the ship; and if the soldiers rebel, you tie the general up and give him over to the enemy. So, too, if you remove marriage from its honored place, you forfeit the glory of celibacy.

I agree that celibacy is good. I say, too, that it is even better than marriage. And, if you wish, I will add that it is as much better than marriage as heaven is better than earth —

as much better as the angels are better than people. If I could find a way to say it still more emphatically, I would.

For the angels "neither marry nor are given in marriage" (Mt 22:30); but they do not spend their days on earth, nor are they troubled by passions, nor do they need food or drink. Music does not appeal to them; nor can a beautiful face sway them. Their natures necessarily remain transparent and bright, untroubled by passion, like a clear and cloudless sky at midday.

Human nature is inferior to these blessed spirits, and yet it strains eagerly, beyond its limits, to match the angels. How? Angels neither marry nor are given in marriage; the same is true of those who make a promise of celibacy. The angels stand constantly before God (see Mt 18:10) and serve Him; and so does the celibate man or woman. If they are unable just now to ascend to heaven like the angels because their body holds them back, they will have much consolation, even in this world, because they receive the Master of the heavens if they are holy in body and spirit.

Do you see the value of celibacy? It makes those who pass their days on earth live like the angels in heaven.

Take It to Prayer

⤜✑⤏

Whoever praises marriage makes celibacy more attractive and luminous.

Is marriage a good thing? Certainly. But then celibacy is more attractive because it is a better thing.

In the celibate life, human nature strains eagerly, beyond its limits, to match the angels.

Learn It by Heart

Celibacy makes those who pass their days on earth live like the angels in heaven.

Apply It to Your Life

Cultivate an appreciation for celibacy, not as a negative choice — "giving up" something good — but as a positive virtue — choosing something better.

41

St. John Chrysostom

Everyone's Father, Earth's Ambassador

Theologians explain that when a man is ordained to the priesthood, he undergoes an "ontological change" — a change in his very being. He is conformed to Christ in a special way. He is "another Christ"; he acts "in the person of Christ" within the Church community, most especially in the sacraments.

The priest's relations with his people involve plenty of difficulty. But his difficulties are nothing compared with his relations with God. These require greater and more thorough earnestness. For he acts as ambassador on behalf of the whole city — and why should I stop at the city? — he acts as ambassador on behalf of the whole world. He prays that God would be merciful toward the sins of all, not only of the living, but also of the dead.

What kind of man should he be? I think that the outspokenness of Moses and Elijah would be insufficient for that kind of prayer. It's as if he were everyone's father, entrusted with the whole world. He draws near to God, begging that wars may be extinguished everywhere, that unrest may be quelled. He asks for peace and plenty, and a swift deliverance from all the ills that trouble each person, publicly and privately. The priest should, moreover, surpass those for whom he prays, in every way, as rulers should surpass their subjects.

What rank shall we give the man who invokes the Holy Spirit, and offers the most awesome sacrifice of the Mass, and constantly handles the Lord of all? What great purity and what real piety must we demand of him? Think about what kind of hands ought to serve these purposes, and what kind of tongue should utter such words. Shouldn't the soul that receives so great a spirit be purer and holier than anything in the world? During the Mass, angels stand by the priest. The powers of heaven fill the entire sanctuary, all the space round about the altar, in honor of Him who lies on the altar.

I know of a certain old and holy man who saw visions. One time, quite suddenly, he saw — as much as he could — a crowd of angels, clothed in shining robes, encircling the altar. They were bending down, as soldiers do in the presence of their king. For my part, I believe it.

Another person told me — and he himself was an eye-witness to this — that those who are about to die, if they have recently partaken of the mysteries with a clean conscience, are guarded by angels as they take their last breath. And afterward the angels bear them away — all for the sake of the sacrament the dying people have received.

One should tremble to introduce a soul into so sacred a mystery, to advance to the dignity of the priesthood. For the soul of the priest should shine like a light beaming over the whole world.

Take It to Prayer

A priest's difficulties are like nothing compared with his relations with God.

A priest is ambassador on behalf of the whole world, the living and the dead.

A priest is like everyone's father, entrusted with the whole world.

Learn It by Heart

The soul of the priest should shine like a light beaming over the whole world.

Apply It to Your Life

Honor the priests you know, for what they do and for who they are — not, perhaps, by the strength of their own virtues, but because of the grace God has given them. By the words of consecration, He has changed them, as surely as He changes bread to His body in the Eucharist. Before we correct a priest, we should pray and fast for him. And, if we must correct him, we should do so privately, as much as possible.

42

St. John Chrysostom

Those Holy Hands

Every priest works with consecrated hands — hands blessed by God for the administration of heavenly things, even during earthly life.

The priestly duty is carried out on earth, but it ranks among heavenly things. For neither man nor angel nor archangel nor any other created power established this vocation, but the Holy Spirit Himself. He persuaded men to represent the ministry of angels while still abiding in the flesh. This is why the consecrated priest ought to be as pure as if he were standing amid those powers in heaven. For when you see the Lord sacrificed and laid upon the altar, and the priest standing in prayer over the victim, and all the worshipers' lips stained with the precious blood, can you then think that you are still in human company, still standing on earth? Aren't you, rather, immediately taken to heaven? Casting every fleshly thought from your soul, don't you, with spirit and pure reason, contemplate the things that are in heaven?

What a marvel! What love God has for us! He who sits on high with the Father is then held in the hands of everyone, and He gives Himself to those who are willing to embrace and hold Him.

Picture Elijah and the vast crowd standing around, and the sacrifice laid upon the altar of stones, and all the rest of the people hushed in a deep silence while the prophet alone prays. Then comes the sudden rush of fire from heaven upon the sacrifice.

Now pass from that scene to the rites that are celebrated today. These are not only marvelous to see, but awe-inspiring. There stands the priest, not bringing down fire from heaven, but the Holy Spirit! And he prays a long time, not that some flame may descend and consume the offerings, but that grace may descend on the sacrifice and thereby inflame the souls of all, and make them more brilliant than silver purified by fire.

Who can belittle this most awesome mystery, unless he is stark mad and senseless? Don't you know that without the help of God's grace, no human soul could have endured that fire in the sacrifice, but all would have been utterly consumed?

Consider how great it is for a man, mere flesh and blood, to be able to approach that blessed and pure nature. Then you must clearly see what a great honor the Spirit's grace has given to priests. By their action these rites are celebrated, and other actions that are in no way inferior to these pertaining to our redemption and salvation.

Those who live on earth are entrusted to administer the things that are in heaven. They have received authority that God has not given to angels or archangels. For it is not to them that God said: "Whatever you bind on earth shall be bound in heaven, and whatever you loose on earth shall be loosed in heaven" (Mt 18:18). Those who rule on earth have authority to bind, but only the body; this bond, though, lays hold of the soul and penetrates the heavens. What priests do here below, God ratifies above, and the Master confirms the sentence of His servants. For indeed it is heavenly authority He gives them when He says: "If you forgive the sins of any, they are forgiven; if you retain the sins of any, they are retained" (Jn 20:23). What authority could be greater than this?

"The Father … has given all judgment to the Son" (Jn 5:22). But I see it all put into the hands of these men by the Son. For no one can enter into the kingdom of heaven unless he is born again through water and the Spirit, and he who does not eat the flesh of the Lord and drink His blood is excluded from eternal life — and all these things take place only by means of those holy hands, the hands of the priest. How, then, will anyone, without the help of these hands, be able to escape the fire of hell, or to win those crowns that are reserved for the victorious?

Take It to Prayer

When you see the Lord sacrificed and laid upon the altar, aren't you immediately taken to heaven?

What love God has for us! He who sits on high with the Father is held in the hands of everyone.

Without God's grace, no human soul could have endured
that fire in the sacrifice of the Mass, but all would have been
utterly consumed.

Learn It by Heart

~≫≪~

What priests do here below, God ratifies above.

Apply It to Your Life

~≫≪~

Pray for priests. St. John holds them to a high standard,
expecting each "to be as pure as if he were standing ... in
heaven." Priests also face high expectations from their
parishioners and their bishop. But no one expects as much
from them as God does. The good news is that He has the
power to give them whatever He asks of them, and He will
not ask anything they cannot give back, with His help. If the
priesthood is in crisis today, it is not time for anyone to
blame the priests. Constructive criticism should begin at
home, with a sober evaluation of how much and how often
we've sacrificed for God's priests, prayed for them, and
treated them kindly — beginning with the ones we like the
least.

with St. Leo the Great

The Glory of God, The Glory of Us All

St. Leo I (d. 461) is one of only two popes who bear the title "the Great" alongside their name. Yet we know little about his personal life. We have no idea, for example, when he was born. Though he left behind voluminous official correspondence and sermons, he hardly ever mentioned himself. Perhaps his true greatness was his profound humility. Though he occupied the most prestigious office on earth, Leo's life was truly "hid with Christ in God" (Col 3:3).

He was born and raised in Rome, ordained to the priesthood in Rome, and served as an official under two of his papal predecessors. At the time he was elected pope, in the year 440, Leo was hundreds of miles away, in another country on Church business.

On his return he was crowned, and he established himself immediately as a teaching bishop. He preached ninety-six sermons on Christian doctrine, refuting the most common errors of his time. Indeed, several heresies had been a plague upon the Church for centuries. The bishops of the world had met three times in council to condemn errant doctrine, but the heresies endured.

In 449, St. Leo wrote his most important work, his *Tome*, which lays out, in a series of propositions, the Church's teaching on the Trinity and on Christ's full divinity, true humanity, and dual natures. The language was stark and precise. If

Leo had had his way, nothing would be left to speculation, doubt, or debate. In 451, the Council of Chalcedon proclaimed Leo's *Tome* as a dogmatic statement, saying: "Peter has spoken through Leo."

Pope Leo is perhaps most famous for his negotiation with Attila the Hun, turning back the barbarian and his army when they were at the gates of Rome. When the Vandals sacked Rome in 455, Leo persuaded them not to burn the city.

Through his life on earth, Leo merited the titles "pope," "saint," and "great." At his death, in 461, he went to his true reward.

Throughout St. Leo's preaching, he shows a singular fascination for the "mysteries" of Christ. The mysteries are eternal: Veiled in the Old Testament, signified in the New, they will be fully revealed only in glory, in eternity. The Old Testament spoke of the Savior "under the veil of mysteries." And even today, the events of Jesus' earthly life "have passed over into His mysteries." What St. Augustine taught in his theology of signs, we find implicit through all of St. Leo's work. The visible sign tells us of the invisible and divine realities.

The time from Easter to Pentecost, says Pope Leo, is the Church's special time for revealing mysteries. In this, the Church follows Christ, who used that same time for the mystagogy of His disciples.

43

St. Leo the Great

Living History

Leo's teaching on the mysteries finds compact expression in a single line from this homily: "All that Jesus did and taught, we not only know as a matter of past history, but appreciate in the power of its effects today." Jesus' saving actions were not intended only for a long-ago people in a faraway place. He established the sacraments so that every generation and every people could participate just as directly in His saving mysteries.

All that the Son of God did and taught for reconciling the world, we not only know as a matter of past history, but appreciate in the power of its effects today.

It is He who, born of the Virgin Mother by the Holy Spirit, fertilizes His spotless Church with the same blessed Spirit, so that by the birth of baptism a countless multitude of children may be born to God — "born, not of blood nor of the will of the flesh nor of the will of man, but of God" (Jn 1:13).

It is He in whom the seed of Abraham is blessed by the adoption of the whole world (see Rom 4:12-18). And so the patriarch has become the father of nations, the children of the promise, born not of flesh but faith.

It is He who, without excluding any nation, makes one flock of holy sheep from every nation under heaven, and every day fulfills His promise: "I have other sheep, that are not of this fold; I must bring them also, and they will heed my voice. So there shall be one flock, one shepherd" (Jn 10:16). To blessed Peter first and foremost He says, "Feed my sheep" (Jn 21:17). Yet the one Lord directs the duties of all the shepherds, and He feeds those who come to the Rock with such pleasant and well-watered pastures, that countless sheep are nourished by the richness of His love. They do not hesitate to die for the Shepherd's sake, even as the Good Shepherd Himself was willing to lay down His life for His sheep (see Jn 10:15).

It is He whose sufferings are shared not only by the martyrs' glorious courage, but also in the very act of rebirth by the faith of all the newborn.

With the renunciation of the devil and belief in God, we pass from the old state into new life. We cast off the earthly image, and put on the heavenly form. All this is a sort of dying and rising. And those who are received by Christ and receive Christ are not the same afterward as they were before they came to the baptismal font, for the bodies reborn become the flesh of the Crucified.

This change, dearly beloved, is the work of the Most High, who works all things in all (see 1 Cor 12:6). By the good way of life seen in each of the faithful, we recognize the Author of all good works, and we give thanks to God's mercy. For He adorns the whole body of the Church with countless gifts of grace. Through many rays, the one Light shines with the same brightness everywhere. Thus, anything done well by any Christian must be part of the glory of Christ.

This is that true light that justifies and enlightens everyone. This is what rescues us from the power of darkness and brings us into the kingdom of the Son of God. This is the newness of life that elevates the desires of the mind and quenches the lusts of the flesh. This is how the Lord's Passover is duly kept, "with the unleavened bread of sincerity and truth," and by casting away "the old leaven, the leaven of malice and evil" (1 Cor 5:8). The new creature eats and drinks from the Lord Himself. For by sharing in the body and blood of Christ, we pass over into what we have received. In Him and with Him we died, and were buried and rose again. Let us, then, both in spirit and in body, carry Him everywhere. As the apostle says, "For you have died, and your life is hid with Christ in God. When Christ who is our life appears, then you also will appear with him in glory" (Col 3:3-4). For He lives and reigns with the Father and the Holy Spirit, forever and ever. Amen.

Take It to Prayer

We pass from the old state into new life. We cast off the earthly image and put on the heavenly form. All this is a sort of dying and rising.

By sharing in the body and blood of Christ, we pass over into what we have received.

Christ's sufferings are shared not only by the martyrs' glorious courage, but also in the very act of rebirth by the faith of all the newborn.

Learn It by Heart

After you come to the baptismal font, your body reborn becomes the flesh of the Crucified.

Apply It to Your Life

Christ acted "without excluding any nation." We, too, must be all–inclusive in our witness. Examine your life: Are there people you consider exempt from your kindness? Are you cold toward some people because they annoy you or they have offended you? You cannot enjoy communion with Christ while you are denying charity to others.

44

St. Leo the Great

The Old and the New

God's plan and its ultimate fulfillment were evident throughout sacred history. Prophets foresaw and foretold the coming of Jesus, His salvation, and His sacramental mysteries. The radiant fulfillment of the Gospel casts the shadow of Christ backward onto every page of the Old Testament.

O wondrous power of the cross! O ineffable glory of the passion! In this is the Lord's tribunal, the world's judgment, and the power of the Crucified! For you drew all things to Yourself, Lord, and when You had stretched out Your hands all day long to an unbelieving and rebellious people (see Is 65:2), the whole world at last was brought to confess Your majesty.

You drew all things to Yourself, Lord, when all the elements combined to pronounce judgment on the crime of Your crucifixion: when the lights of heaven were darkened, and the day turned into night, and the earth was shaken with unusual shocks, and all creation refused to serve the wicked deed. You drew all things to Yourself, Lord, for the veil of the temple was torn in two, and the Holy of Holies existed no more for unworthy high priests: so that the sign was turned into truth, prophecy into manifestation, law into Gospel.

You drew all things to Yourself, Lord, so that what before was done obscurely in only one Judean temple was now to be celebrated everywhere by the piety of all nations in full and open ritual.

For now there is a nobler rank of Levites, there are elders of greater dignity and priests of holier anointing — because Your cross is the fount of all blessings, the source of all graces, and through it the believers receive strength for weakness, glory for shame, life for death. Now that the variety of animal sacrifices has ceased, the one offering of Your body and blood fulfills all the many kinds of offering. You are the true Lamb of God who takes away the sins of the world, and so You perfect all mysteries in Yourself. As one sacrifice is made instead of many victims, so there is but one kingdom for all nations.

What could be more stable, what could be more firm than this Word, in whose proclamation the trumpets of both the Old and New Testaments resound together, as the writings of the ancient witnesses combine with the teaching of the Gospel? For the pages of both covenants confirm each other. He who had been promised before, under the veil of mysteries, was displayed clearly and conspicuously on the day of His transfiguration by the splendor of the present glory. Because, as blessed John says, "the law was given through Moses; grace and truth came through Jesus Christ" (Jn 1:17). In Him are the fulfillment of both the promise of prophecy and the precepts of the law. For by His presence He teaches the truth of prophecy, and by grace He makes it possible for us to fulfill the commands.

Let everyone's faith, then, be established according to the preaching of the most holy Gospel, and let no one be ashamed of Christ's cross, through which the world was redeemed.

Take It to Prayer

What before was done obscurely in only one Judean temple was now to be celebrated everywhere by the piety of all nations in full and open ritual.

Your cross is the fount of all blessings, the source of all graces, and through it the believers receive strength for weakness, glory for shame, life for death.

The sign was turned into truth, prophecy into manifestation, law into Gospel.

Learn It by Heart

You are the true Lamb of God who takes away the sins of the world, and so You perfect all mysteries in Yourself.

Apply It to Your Life

Make yourself familiar with the Old Testament, the first and the larger portion of the Holy Bible. There, in words inspired by God, yet under the veil of mystery, we find the promise of Christ, His cross, His truth, His Eucharist. Faith, for us, lifts the veil if we commit ourselves to sustained, disciplined, prayerful study.

45

St. Leo the Great

Jesus Lingered for Us

St. Leo explains why Jesus waited forty days before ascending to the Father. During this time, His disciples' eyes were opened, as ours are, too, in mystagogy.

Almost forty days have passed, dearly beloved, since the blessed and glorious resurrection of Our Lord Jesus Christ, when the divine power in three days raised the true Temple of God, which wickedness had overthrown (see Jn 2:19). This divinely ordained span of forty days was devoted to our practical instruction. The Lord lingered in His body during this prolonged time so that our faith in the resurrection might be strengthened by needed evidence.

For Christ's death had greatly disturbed the disciples' hearts. His torture on the cross, His last breath, and the burial of His lifeless body had left their grief-stricken minds sluggish with distrust. The Gospel tells us that the holy women brought word that the stone had been rolled away from the tomb, that the body was gone, and that the angels had borne witness to the living Lord. Yet these words seemed crazy to the apostles and other disciples (see Lk 24:1-11).

The Spirit of Truth would certainly not have permitted such doubt, coming from human weakness, to exist in His own preachers' hearts, unless their trembling anxiety and cautious delay were to lay the foundations of our faith. It was our confusions and our dangers that were provided for in the apostles. It was we ourselves who in these men were taught how to meet the objections of the ungodly and the arguments of earthly wisdom. We are instructed by their seeing. Their hearing taught us. Their touching convinced us. Let us give thanks to the divine plan and the holy fathers' necessary slowness to believe. Others doubted, so that we might not doubt.

Dearly beloved, the days that passed between the Lord's resurrection and ascension did not pass by in uneventful leisure. Great mysteries were confirmed in those days, and deep truths were revealed. Those days removed the fear of awful death and established the immortality not only of the soul, but also of the flesh.

In those days, when the Lord breathed upon them, the Holy Spirit was poured upon all the apostles, and the care of the Lord's flock was entrusted to the blessed apostle Peter (Jn 21:15-17), who had already received the keys of the kingdom (see Mt 16:19).

It was then that the Lord joined the two disciples as a companion on their way (Lk 24:13-31); and, to wipe away all the clouds of our doubt, He rebuked the slowness of their fearful hearts. Their enlightened hearts caught the flame of faith and, lukewarm as they had been, began to burn while the Lord unfolded the Scriptures. In the breaking of bread, too, their eyes were opened as they ate with Him.

How much more blessed was the opening of their eyes, at the revelation of their glorified nature, than the opening of our first parents' eyes, when they saw the disastrous consequences of their sin (see Gen 3:7).

Take It to Prayer

Great mysteries were confirmed in those days between the Lord's resurrection and ascension, and deep truths were revealed.

The apostles' trembling anxiety and cautious delay laid the foundations of our faith.

We are instructed by their seeing, convinced by their touching.

Learn It by Heart

Give thanks for the holy apostles' slowness to believe. Others doubted, so that we might not doubt.

Apply It to Your Life

God has His reasons for allowing people to wait a while in unbelief and sadness. When you are praying for another person's conversion, be persistent, but be patient, too. Remember the apostles.

46

St. Leo the Great

Ascend with Jesus

Christ's ascension marked the exaltation of our human nature. We saw ourselves divinized when our nature rose to glory in the person of Jesus.

Amidst these miracles, when the disciples were troubled by anxieties, the Lord appeared in their midst and said, "Peace be with you" (Jn 20:26). So that what was passing through their hearts might not remain. For they thought they saw a ghost, but He showed that their thoughts were wrong. He showed their doubting eyes the marks of the cross still in His hands and feet, and invited them to touch Him with careful scrutiny. For the traces of the nails and spear had been kept in order to heal the wounds of unbelieving hearts. Thus, not with wavering faith but with steadfast knowledge, they might understand that the nature that had lain in the tomb was soon to sit on God the Father's throne.

So, dearly beloved, throughout this time that passed between the Lord's resurrection and ascension, God's providence had this in mind, taught this, and impressed it upon both the eyes and hearts of His people: that the Lord Jesus Christ might be recognized as truly risen, just as He was truly born, truly suffered, and truly died. That's why the blessed apostles and all the disciples — fearful as they had been at His death on the cross, and hesitant in believing His resurrection — were so strengthened by the clear truth that, when the Lord entered the heights of heaven, not only were they untouched by sadness, but were even filled with great joy.

The cause of their rejoicing was truly great and indescribable when, in the sight of the heavenly multitude, our human nature ascended above the dignity of all heavenly creatures, passing the ranks of the angels and rising beyond the archangels' heights. This ascension was unlimited by any elevation, till our nature was received to sit with the Eternal Father, joined to the throne of His glory, as His divine nature was joined to human nature in the Son.

Since then, Christ's ascension is our exaltation. For there is hope that the body will be raised to the glory where the head has gone before. So, dearly beloved, let us rejoice with delight in our holy thanksgiving. For on the day of the ascension we have not only been confirmed as possessors of paradise, but in Christ we have even pierced through to the heights of heaven. We have gained much greater things through Christ's indescribable grace than we had lost through the devil's malice. Those whom our raging enemy had driven away from the bliss of our first home, the Son of God has made members of Himself and placed at the right hand of the Father, with whom He lives and reigns in the unity of the Holy Spirit, God forever and ever. Amen.

Take It to Prayer

We have gained much greater things through Christ's inde-scribable grace than we had lost through the devil's malice.

When Jesus ascended to heaven, our human nature rose above the dignity of all heavenly creatures, passing the ranks of the angels and archangels.

Our nature was received to sit with the Eternal Father, joined to the throne of His glory, as His divine nature was joined to human nature in the Son.

Learn It by Heart

Christ's ascension is our exaltation. For there is hope that the body will be raised to the glory where the head has gone before.

Apply It to Your Life

Meditate often on heaven. Now that you are divinized in Christ, it is your one true home. A child of God, you can find rest only in the life of the Trinity. Yet that life begins now, in mystery, in the sacraments. You rise to heaven when you confess the sins that weigh you down. Your Commu-nion is in heaven when you go to Mass.

47

St. Leo the Great

The Strength of Faith

From this sermon, delivered on Ascension Thursday in the year 445, the Church has taken its official teaching on the sacramental mysteries, enshrined in the Catechism of the Catholic Church, *n. 1115.*

The mystery of our salvation, dearly beloved, which the Creator of the universe valued at the price of His blood, has now been completed under the conditions of His humiliation — from the day of His bodily birth to the end of His suffering. Although many signs of His divinity shone through, even in the form of a slave (see Phil 2:7), still the events of all that time served particularly to show the reality of the humanity He assumed. But with His suffering, the chains of death were broken, exposed by attacking Him who "knew no sin" (2 Cor 5:21). Then weakness was turned into power, mortality into eternity, disgrace into glory.

The Lord Jesus Christ showed this "by many proofs" (Acts 1:3), before many witnesses, until He carried into heaven the triumphant victory that He had won over death.

On Easter, the Lord's resurrection was the cause of our rejoicing. Now the reason for our gladness is His ascension.

Now we commemorate and honor that day when our humble nature was raised in Christ above all the host of heaven — above all the ranks of angels, beyond the height of all heavenly powers — to sit with God the Father. On this providential order of events, we are established and built up, so that God's grace might become more wonderful when these awesome things are removed from sight, and still faith does not fail, hope does not waver, love does not grow cold.

This is the strength of great minds and the light of souls that are firm in faith: to believe, without hesitation, what is invisible to bodily sight, and to fix the affections where you cannot direct your gaze. From where does this godliness spring up in our hearts; or how should we be "justified by faith" (Rom 5:1), if our salvation depended only on things that stand before our eyes? When a man persisted in doubt of Christ's resurrection until he had tested by sight and touch the traces of suffering in His very flesh, Our Lord said to him, "Have you believed because you have seen me? Blessed are those who have not seen and yet believe" (Jn 20:29).

So that we may be capable of this blessedness, dearly beloved, when all things were fulfilled concerning the Gospel and the mysteries of the New Testament, our Lord Jesus Christ, on the fortieth day after the resurrection, in the sight of the disciples, was raised into heaven. Thus He ended His bodily presence with us, to dwell at the Father's right hand until the time divinely appointed for multiplying the Church's children. He will come to judge the living and the dead in the same flesh in which He ascended.

Now, what was visible in our Savior has passed over into His mysteries. So that faith might be greater and stronger, sight gave way to doctrine. And the authority of this doctrine is accepted by believing hearts enlightened with rays from above.

This faith, increased by the Lord's ascension and established by the gift of the Holy Spirit, was not terrified by chains, imprisonment, exile, hunger, fire, attacks by wild beasts, or the tortures of cruel persecutors. For this faith, throughout the world, men, women, and children fought to the point of shedding their blood. This faith cast out demons, drove away sickness, raised the dead.

The blessed apostles — after being assured by so many miracles and taught by so many discourses — had still been panic-stricken by the horrors of the Lord's passion and had not accepted the truth of His resurrection without hesitation. Yet they made such progress after the Lord's ascension that everything that had previously filled them with fear now turned into joy. For they had raised the whole mind in contemplation to the divinity of Him who sat at the Father's right hand. They were no longer hindered by the obstacle of bodily sight from directing their minds' gaze toward Him who had never left the Father's side when He descended to earth, nor forsaken the disciples when He ascended to heaven.

Take It to Prayer

This is the strength of great minds and the light of souls that are firm in faith: to believe, without hesitation, what is invisible to bodily sight.

So that faith might be greater and stronger, sight gave way to doctrine.

This faith, increased by the Lord's ascension, was not terrified by the tortures of cruel persecutors. For this faith, men, women, and children fought to the point of shedding their blood.

Learn It by Heart

Now, what was visible in our Savior has passed over into His mysteries.

Apply It to Your Life

We may pray for miracles, but we must not lose faith when miracles don't come. Christ performed many miracles so that we might have faith, and that faith has been tested and proved by the willingness of many martyrs to suffer and die. We, too, may have to suffer and die. We may also have to face the suffering and death of people we love. Our faith in

Christ's mysteries will carry us through and have no need of further miracles, even though we desire them with an aching heart.

48

St. Leo the Great

A Better Way of Knowing

Jesus' ascension was not an abandonment of His disciples. It was their elevation to a truer and greater way of knowing Him.

Dearly beloved: When He returned to the glory of the Father's majesty, the Son of Man and Son of God reached a more excellent and holy fame. In an inexpressible way, He began to be nearer to the divinity as He became more remote from our humanity. A better-formed faith then began to draw closer to the Son's equality with the Father, without needing to touch the bodily substance in Christ, by which He is inferior to the Father. Now the nature of the glorified body remained, and the faith of believers was drawn to touch the Only-begotten, who is equal with the Father. They did not, however, touch Him with the hand of flesh, but with spiritual understanding.

This is why when Mary Magdalene (representing the Church) ran to touch our Lord, He said to her: "Do not touch me, for I have not yet ascended to my Father" (see Jn 20:17, CCD). That is to say: "I don't want you to come to Me as if to a human body, or recognize Me by perceptions of the flesh. I am taking you to higher things. I am preparing greater things for you. When I have ascended to My Father, then you shall handle Me more perfectly and truly, for you shall grasp what you cannot now touch and believe what you cannot see."

The disciples' eyes followed the ascending Lord to heaven with upward gaze of earnest wonder. Two angels stood by them in bright, shining garments, and they said, "Men of Galilee, why do you stand looking into heaven? This Jesus, who was taken up from you into heaven, will come in the same way as you saw Him go into heaven" (Acts 1:11). By these words all the Church's children were taught to believe that Jesus Christ will come visibly in the same flesh with which He ascended. We were taught not to doubt that all things are under the authority of Him, whom angels had served from the time of His birth. As an angel announced to the Blessed Virgin that Christ should be conceived by the Holy Spirit, so the voice of heavenly beings sang to the shepherds that He was born of the Virgin. As messengers from above were the first to testify that He rose from the dead, so the angels foretold His coming in flesh to judge the world. Thus we should conclude that great powers will come with Him when He comes to judge, when so many served Him as He was being judged.

Take It to Prayer

⚜

"I don't want you to recognize Me by perceptions of the flesh. I am taking you to higher things. For you shall grasp what you cannot now touch and believe what you cannot see."

Now all things are under the authority of Him, whom angels had served from the time of His birth.

Jesus Christ will come visibly in the same flesh with which He ascended.

Learn It by Heart

⚜

They did not touch Him with the hand of flesh, but with spiritual understanding.

Apply It to Your Life

⚜

Right now — in the sacramental signs of baptism and the Eucharist — your senses perceive what your senses can handle. The signs reveal God to you even as they seem to conceal Him from sight. Through your lifetime of sacramental grace, God will extend your capacity to behold Him, preparing you for glories that your eyes have not seen before, nor could they, your ears have not heard before, nor could they. Ponder the signs, thank God for the signs, but live for the day when you will behold the glory.

49

St. Leo the Great

Pilgrims on Earth

St. Leo urges us to see heaven as our true home and to live here as if we were just passing through. These are the marching orders that mystagogy gives us. We are to live in the afterglow of the ascension and in anticipation of Jesus' coming. We proclaim in every Mass: "Christ will come again!" And He comes to us again, in every Mass!

And so, dearly beloved, let's rejoice with spiritual joy, and let's gladly give God the thanks He is due. Let us freely raise the eyes of our hearts to those heights where Christ is. Hearts that have heard the call to be lifted up must not be held down by earthly desires. Those who are made for things eternal must not be occupied with the things that perish. Those who have begun the way of truth must not become entangled in the snares of falsehood. The faithful must make their way through these temporal things, keeping in mind that they are pilgrims in the valley of this world; and, even though they find some attractions along the way, they must not sinfully embrace them, but bravely pass them by.

When the blessed apostle Peter made his threefold profession of love for the Lord, he conceived a desire to feed Christ's sheep (see Jn 21:15-17). And it is according to that desire that he eagerly begs: "Beloved, I beseech you as aliens and exiles to abstain from the passions of the flesh that wage war against your soul" (1 Pet 2:11). But on whose side do the passions of the flesh wage war? On the devil's side, for he delights in chaining souls that strive after higher things. He chains them with the enticements of corruptible goods, and he draws them away from those places from which he himself has been banished. Every believer must keep careful watch against his plots, so that he may crush the enemy on the side where the attack is made.

Dearly beloved, there is no more powerful weapon against the devil's wiles than kind mercy and generous love. By these, every sin can be escaped or defeated. But this lofty power is not reached until its opposition has been overthrown. And what is so hostile to works of mercy and charity as greed, the root of all evil (see 1 Tim 6:10)? Unless this is destroyed and left without nourishment, this evil weed will take root in the ground of the heart, and the thorns and briars of vices will rise up, rather than any seed of true goodness.

Let's resist this deadly evil and "aim at charity" (see 1 Cor 14:1, CCD), for without this no virtue can flourish. By this path of love, Christ came down to us; by it, we, too, may ascend to Him. And to Him, with God the Father and the Holy Spirit, be honor and glory forever and ever. Amen.

Take It to Prayer

The faithful are pilgrims in this world; and, though they find attractions along the way, they must not sinfully embrace them, but bravely pass them by. Those who are made for things eternal must not be occupied with things that perish.

The devil chains souls with the enticements of corruptible goods, and he draws them away from those places from which he himself has been banished.

Unless greed is destroyed, this evil weed will take root in the heart, and the thorns and briars of vices will rise up, rather than any seed of true goodness.

Learn It by Heart

Aim at charity. By this path of love, Christ came down to us; by it, we, too, may ascend to Him.

Apply It to Your Life

We cannot ascend to God if we are weighed down by the things of earth. God made the things of this world to be samples of His glory. Indeed, He chose some earthly goods — food and wine and fragrant oil — to be sacramental signs of His presence and power. The things of this world are good, but our desires for them have been disordered by sin. We make sensual delight an end in itself, and so we make it an idol, a master, who rules us by our bad habits and addictions. We must restore order to our eating, drinking, and other bodily pleasures. We must discipline ourselves often by denying ourselves some of the pleasures we desire. Our bodies want more than they need, so we should give them less than they want. Once disciplined, our bodily desire itself will serve as a sign of the desire of our souls. Thus relieved of our earthly attachments, we can rise up to God on high. Thus emptied of earthly desire by our fasting, we can be filled up with God's Holy Spirit.

50

~e9~

St. Leo the Great

The Fire Still Burns

On the first Pentecost, the coming of the Spirit lit up the minds and hearts of thousands. Now they could understand, and now they could speak with understanding, to help others understand. Now, with the fire of the Spirit of Christ, they had pierced the veil of the mysteries. This fire blazed from person to person to consume whole families and, soon, entire lands. The Holy Spirit had come to renew the face of the earth.

Every Catholic knows, dearly beloved, that today's solemnity should be counted among the principal feasts. No one questions the respect due to the day the Spirit made holy by the miraculous gift of Himself. This is the tenth day from the day when the Lord ascended to sit at the right hand of God the Father in heaven. It is the fiftieth day from His resurrection.

Pentecost holds great mysteries in itself, mysteries new and old. By them it is clear that grace was foretold through the old law, and the old law was fulfilled through grace. When the Hebrew people were freed from the Egyptians, the law was given on Mount Sinai on the fiftieth day after the sacrifice of the lambs. So, after the suffering of Christ — the true Lamb of God, who was slain — and on the fiftieth day from His resurrection, the Holy Spirit came down upon the apostles and the crowd of believers. The true Christian can easily see how the beginnings of the Old Testament prepared for the beginnings of the Gospel, and that the second covenant was founded by the same Spirit who had set up the first.

The apostles' story testifies: "When the day of Pentecost had come, they were all together in one place. And suddenly a sound came from heaven like the rush of a mighty wind, and it filled all the house where they were sitting. And there appeared to them tongues as of fire, distributed and resting on each one of them. And they were all filled with the Holy Spirit and began to speak in other tongues, as the Spirit gave them utterance" (Acts 2:1-4).

Oh, how swift are the words of wisdom! How quickly the lesson is learned when God is the teacher! No interpretation is needed for understanding, no practice for using, no time for studying. The Spirit of Truth blows where He wills (see Jn 3:8), and the languages of each nation become common property in the mouth of the Church. So, from that day, the Gospel preaching has resounded like a trumpet. From that day, the showers of gracious gifts, the rivers of blessings, have watered every desert and all the dry land. To "renew the face of the earth" (Ps 104:30, CCD), the Spirit of God "was moving over the face of the waters" (Gen 1:2); and to drive away the old darkness, flashes of new light shone forth. By the blaze of those busy tongues, the Lord's bright Word kindled speech into fire — fire to arouse the understanding and to consume sin. Fire has the power to enlighten and the power to burn.

God's Word has authority, and it is ablaze with these and countless other proofs. Let us, all together, wake up to celebrate Pentecost. Let's rejoice in honor of the Holy Spirit, through whom the whole Catholic Church is made holy, and every rational soul comes alive. He is the Inspirer of Faith, the Teacher of Knowledge, the Fountain of Love, the Seal of Chastity, and the Source of all Power.

Let the spirits of the faithful rejoice. Let one God — Father, Son, and Holy Spirit — be praised throughout the world, by the confession of all languages. And may that sign of His presence, the likeness of fire, burn perpetually in His work and gift.

The Spirit of Truth makes the house of His glory shine with the brightness of His light, and He wants nothing in His temple to be dark or lukewarm.

Take It to Prayer

Pentecost holds great mysteries, new and old. The beginnings of the Old Testament prepared for the beginnings of the Gospel, and that the second covenant was founded by the same Spirit who had set up the first.

By the blaze of those busy tongues, the Lord's bright Word kindled speech into fire — fire to arouse the understanding and to consume sin. Fire has the power to enlighten and the power to burn.

May that sign of the Spirit's presence, the likeness of fire, burn perpetually in His work and gift.

Learn It by Heart

The Spirit of Truth makes the house of His glory shine with the brightness of His light, and He wants nothing in His temple to be dark or lukewarm.

Apply It to Your Life

All history has been lit up by the fire of the Spirit. The fire burns through every moment of your life now. Remain aware of His presence. See everything by God's light. Let His fire consume your sins. Warm the world by the radiance of His love.

Sources and References

Most selections in this book are adapted from translations in the series *Ante-Nicene Fathers* (ANF) and *A Select Library of Nicene and Post-Nicene Fathers of the Christian Church* (NPNF), edited by Philip Schaff and Henry Wace in the years 1886 to 1900. These series, together, are commonly called the "Edinburgh edition" of the Fathers, after the Scottish university where they originated. All thirty-eight volumes are available in bound form from Hendrickson Publishers (Peabody, Mass.). Electronic editions are available on several websites, including New Advent (www.newadvent.org) and the Christian Classics Ethereal Library (www.ccel.org). The original translations in both series are uneven, the English is archaic, and the introductions and footnotes are sometimes virulently anti-Catholic. More readable translations, and more reliable historical scholarship, can usually be found in the *Fathers of the Church* series (CUA) published by Catholic University of America Press (Washington, D.C.) and the *Ancient Christian Writers* (ACW) series published by Paulist Press (Mahwah, N.J.), as well as in other volumes listed below.

Mystagogical Texts

1. Adapted from *On the Holy Spirit 27*. 66-67. NPNF, series 2, vol. 8.

2. Adapted from *On the Baptism of Christ.* NPNF, series 2, vol. 5.

3. Adapted from *The Great Catechism 35.* NPNF, series 2, vol. 5.

4. Adapted from *Life of Moses,* several translations. Full texts can be found in:

> *From Glory to Glory: Texts from Gregory of Nyssa's Mystical Writings,* selected and with an introduction by Jean Danielou, S.J.; translated and edited by Herbert Musurillo, S.J. New York: Charles Scribner's Sons, 1961.

> *Gregory of Nyssa: The Life of Moses,* translated by Abraham Malherbe and Everett Ferguson, in the *Classics of Western Spirituality* series. New York: Paulist Press, 1978.

5. Adapted from *On the Baptism of Christ.* NPNF, series 2, vol. 5.

6. Adapted from *The Great Catechism 39.* NPNF, series 2, vol. 5.

7. Adapted from *Letter 17, To Eustathia, Ambrosia, and Basilissa.* NPNF, series 2, vol. 5.

8. Adapted from *Catechetical Lectures 19.* NPNF, series 2, vol. 7. Full texts can also be found in:

> *The Awe-Inspiring Rites of Initiation: The Origins of the RCIA,* Edward Yarnold, S.J. Collegeville, Minn.: Liturgical Press, 1994.

> *The Works of Saint Cyril of Jerusalem*, vol. 2, translated by Leo P. McCauley, S.J., and Anthony A. Stephenson in CUA, 1970.

9. Adapted from *Catechetical Lectures 19.* NPNF, series 2, vol. 7. Full texts can also be found in Yarnold and CUA.

10. Adapted from *Catechetical Lectures 20.* NPNF, series 2, vol. 7. Full texts can also be found in Yarnold and CUA.

11. Ibid.

12. Ibid.

13. Adapted from *Catechetical Lectures 21*. NPNF, series 2, vol. 7. Full texts can also be found in Yarnold and CUA.

14. Ibid.

15. Adapted from *Christ the Teacher 1.6*. ANF, vol. 2. Full text can also be found in *Clement of Alexandria: Christ the Educator,* translated by Simon P. Wood, C.P., in CUA, 1954.

16. Ibid.

17. Adapted from *The Stromata 7.17*. ANF, vol. 2.

18. Adapted from *Christ the Teacher 2.2*. ANF, vol. 2. Full text can also be found in CUA.

19. Adapted from *Who is the Rich Man That Shall Be Saved?* ANF, vol. 2.

20. Adapted from "Exhortation to Endurance." Clement of Alexandria, translated by G.W. Butterworth, London-New York: Loeb Classical Library, 1919, pp. 370-377.

21. Adapted from *The Stromata 6.12*. ANF, vol. 2.

22. Adapted from *On the Sacraments 4.1. On the Mysteries and Treatise on the Sacraments,* translated by T. Thompson. Edited by J.H. Strawley. London: SPCK, 1919. Full texts can also be found in Yarnold and *Saint Ambrose: Theological and Dogmatic Works,* CUA, 1963.

23. Adapted from *On the Sacraments 4.3* in Thompson. Full texts can also be found in Yarnold and CUA.

24. Adapted from *On the Sacraments 4.4* and *On the Mysteries 9* in Thompson. Full texts can also be found in Yarnold and CUA.

25. Adapted from *On the Sacraments 4.5* in Thompson. Full texts can also be found in Yarnold and CUA.

26. Adapted from *On the Sacraments 4.6* in Thompson. Full texts can also be found in Yarnold and CUA.

27. Adapted from *On the Sacraments* 5.2-3 in Thompson. Full texts can also be found in Yarnold and CUA.

28. Adapted from *On the Sacraments 5.4* in Thompson. Full texts can also be found in Yarnold and CUA.

29. Adapted from *Sermon 272*. Newly translated from the Latin in Migne's *Patrologia Latina.* Other translations can be found in:

> *The Works of Saint Augustine: A Translation for the 21st Century,* Sermons vol. III/7, translated by Edmund Hill, O.P. New Rochelle, N.Y.: New City Press, 1993.

> *Journey with the Fathers: Commentaries on the Sunday Gospels, Year A,* edited by Edith Barnecut, O.S.B., Hyde Park, N.Y.: New City Press, 1992.

30. Adapted from *Sermon 229.* Newly translated from the Latin in Migne's *Patrologia Latina.* Other translations can be found in *The Works of Saint Augustine* (vol. III/6), and

> *Saint Augustine: Sermons on the Liturgical Seasons,* translated by Sister Mary Sarah Muldowney, R.S.M., CUA, Washington, D.C.: Catholic University of America Press, 1959.

31. Adapted from *Expositions on the Psalms 40.* NPNF, series 1, vol. 8.

32. Adapted from *Expositions on the Psalms 86.* NPNF, series 1, vol. 8.

33. Adapted from *Sermon 223.* Newly translated from the Latin in Migne's *Patrologia Latina.* Other translations can be found in CUA and *The Works of Saint Augustine* (vol. III/6).

34. Adapted from *City of God 20.9.* NPNF, series 1, vol. 2.

35. Adapted from *Sermon 227.* Newly translated from the Latin in Migne's *Patrologia Latina.* Other translations can be found in CUA and *The Works of Saint Augustine.*

36. Adapted from *Homilies on Colossians 12.5.* NPNF, series 1, vol. 13. Other translations can be found in:

St. John Chrysostom: On Marriage and Family Life, translated by Catharine P. Roth and David Anderson, Crestwood, N.Y.: St. Vladimir's Seminary Press, 1986.

The Human Couple in the Fathers, introduction and notes by Giulia Sfameni Gasparro, Cesare Magazzú, and Concetta Aloe Spada; English translation by Thomas Halton. Boston: Pauline Books and Media, 1998.

37. Adapted from *Homilies on Ephesians 20.* NPNF, series 1, vol. 13. Other translations can be found in Roth et al. and Sfameni et al.

38. Ibid.

39. Ibid.

40. Adapted from *On Virginity 10-11.* Full text can be found in *On Virginity, Against Remarriage,* translated by Sally Rieger Shore, *Studies in Women and Religion, vol. 9,* New York: Edwin Mellen Press, 1983.

41. Adapted from *On the Priesthood 6.4.* NPNF, series 1, vol. 9.

42. Adapted from *On the Priesthood 3.4-5.* NPNF, series 1, vol. 9.

43. Adapted from *Sermons 63.6-7.* NPNF, series 2, vol. 12. Another translation can be found in *St. Leo the Great: Sermons,* translated by Jane Patricia Freeland, C.S.J.B., and Agnes Josephine Conway, S.S.J., CUA, 1996.

44. Adapted from *Sermons 59.7, 51.5, 51.8.* NPNF, series 2, vol. 12. Another translation can be found in CUA.

45. Adapted from *Sermons 73.1-2.* NPNF, series 2, vol. 12. Another translation can be found in CUA.

46. Adapted from *Sermons 73.3-4.* NPNF, series 2, vol. 12. Another translation can be found in CUA.

47. Adapted from *Sermons 74.1-3.* NPNF, series 2, vol. 12. Another translation can be found in CUA.

48. Adapted from *Sermons 74.4.* NPNF, series 2, vol. 12. Another translation can be found in CUA.

49. Adapted from *Sermons 74.5.* NPNF, series 2, vol. 12. Another translation can be found in CUA.

50. Adapted from *Sermons 75.1-2,5.* NPNF, series 2, vol. 12. Another translation can be found in CUA.

General Studies

From Darkness to Light: How One Became a Christian in the Early Church, Anne Field, O.S.B., Ben Lomond, Calif.: Conciliar Press, 1997.

The Awe-Inspiring Rites of Initiation: The Origins of the RCIA, Edward Yarnold, S.J. Collegeville, Minn.: Liturgical Press, 1994.

Mystagogy: A Theology of Liturgy in the Patristic Age, Enrico Mazza, New York: Pueblo Publishing, 1989.

The Mystery of Christian Worship, Odo Casel, O.S.B. New York: Crossroad, 1999.

By the Same Authors

The Lamb's Supper: The Mass as Heaven on Earth, Scott Hahn, New York: Doubleday, 1999. A contemporary mystagogy of the Mass.

A Father Who Keeps His Promises: God's Covenant Love in Scripture, Scott Hahn, Ann Arbor, Mich.: Servant, 1998. An introduction to the typological reading of the Bible.

Ignatius Catholic Study Bible, edited by Scott Hahn and Curtis Mitch, San Francisco, Cal.: Ignatius. A series presenting individual books of the Bible with thorough introductions, commentaries, and notes.

The Mass of the Early Christians, Mike Aquilina. Huntington, Ind.: Our Sunday Visitor, 2001. Actual texts of the earliest liturgies.

The Fathers of the Church: An Introduction to the First Christian Teachers, Mike Aquilina. Huntington, Ind.: Our Sunday Visitor, 1999.

The How-To Book of Catholic Devotions, Mike Aquilina and Regis J. Flaherty. Huntington, Ind.: Our Sunday Visitor, 2000. Step-by-step instructions for the Church's traditional prayers and practices.

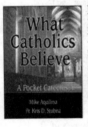